THE CLOCK FLOWER

Also by Adrian Rice

POETRY
Muck Island
Impediments
The Mason's Tongue
Hickory Haiku

NONFICTION
The Tin God

AS EDITOR
Signals
Life of the Lough
Sea & Shore
Around the Lough
A Conversation Piece
    (edited with Angela Reid)
Lough Views
Exploring the Lough: Creative Activities
    for the Primary School Classroom
(edited with Molly Freeman)
Insights
Shore Lines

The Clock Flower

for
Helen Vendler —
with Belfast blessings,
and with admiration for
the work in the books —

Poems

Warmest,

Adrian Rice

Adrian Rice x
11th June, 2015
Hickory

Press 53
Winston-Salem

Press 53, LLC
PO Box 30314
Winston-Salem, NC 27130

First Edition

Copyright © 2013 by Adrian Rice

The Clock Flower was originally published in 2012 by Moongate Publications,
Northern Ireland, in a limited edition of 250 copies.

Cover design by Kevin Morgan Watson

Cover art, "The Seven Ages of Mandelion," Copyright © 2013 by Jon Turner,
used by permission of the artist.

Author photo by Jon Eckard, Eckard Photographic.
www.eckardphotographic.com

Printed on acid-free paper
ISBN 978-1-935708-99-5

For
Molly and Micah
Matthew, Charis and Charlotte

and

Dedicated to
William Matthew Wilson (1960-2009)
Brother – Friend – Helper – Protector

A Note from the Publisher

The Clock Flower was first published by Moongate Publications of Northern Ireland in 2012 in a limited edition printing of 250 copies. In publishing this new edition, by a United States publisher, we chose to honor United Kingdom grammar and punctuation styles, for example, not moving commas and periods inside the quotation marks, and by not dropping or changing letters from certain words, as our way of preserving the integrity, charm and spirit of the poems and the voice of the poet.

ACKNOWLEDGMENTS

The author and the publisher gratefully acknowledge the following for previous hospitality to some of these poems:

"The Recovery," and "The Apologist" first appeared in *Poetry Ireland Review*

"The Book of Life," "The Grieving Ground," and "The Changeful Tap" first appeared under the title 'Sorrow Songs' in *The Mason's Tongue* (Abbey Press, 1999)

"The Book of Life" also appeared in a special Irish Poetry issue of *Chapman*

"The Changeful Tap" was also included in the anthology *Magnetic North: The Emerging Poets* (Verbal Arts Centre/Lagan Press, 2006), ed. John Brown

"Whale," "Among The Lavender," "Bullets Or Bats," and "The Clock Flower" first appeared in *Iodine Poetry Journal*

"Ever Émigrés," "Just Enough," and "Neighbourhood" first appeared in *The Echo Room*

Some of the poems were broadcast in N. Ireland/Ireland on BBC Radio Ulster, Lyric FM, RTE's *Arena* with Sean Rocks, and in America on *First Talk* with Hal Row (WHKY), and *Wordplay* with Jeff Davis (Asheville FM)

The author would also like to thank a host of other encouragers: Sacha Abercorn (The Duchess of Abercorn), Kerry Adamson, Nathalie Anderson, Lindsay Barrick, Martin Beattie, Michael Beattie, Rand & Beth Brandes, Gregory Burton (U.S. Consul General in Belfast), Barbara Burns, Robert Canipe, Brendan Cleary, Roger Cooke, Paul Custer, Duane Davis, Mary Rowe Dethlefs, Sammy Douglas (MLA), Michael & Barbara Dugan, Ian Duhig, Sally Fanjoy & James Labrenz, Ramona Fletcher, Keith Flynn, Seth Collings Hawkins, Marie Heaney, Brian Houston, Kenneth Irvine, Brendan Kennelly, Andrew Licout, Marion Love & Keith Wood, Mel McMahon, Dorothy Maguire, Chrisanne & Lamar Mitchell, Annie Nice, Betty Orr, Glenn Patterson, Eve Patton, Tim Peeler, Martin Quinn, Michael Rawl, Anne Rawson, Jonathan K. Rice, Mark Roper, Richard R. Russell, Jerry Sain, Ari Sigal, Angela Beaver Simmons, Kevin Smith, Sandy & Mike Stevenson, and especially Kevin Morgan Watson and Christine Norris at Press 53.

Very special, heart-full thanks are due to Ross Wilson, the *sine qua non* – "186." Fellow Belfastman, Alan Mearns, my Hickory-stationed "mucker" and fellow "dartist," has been a tireless and peerless critical helpmate – three poems here have him as dedicee, which I trust signals my deepest gratitude. Back home, John Orr has also provided timely encouragement, and has cast a similar, necessary, "cold eye." My poet son, Matthew, has been an important poem-goader and inspiration. I also want to acknowledge my supportive mother, and my brother Arran, not least for shipping my books back to me. Love goes out to them both; and to my brother Annesley; and to my father. To my wife and kids: Molly, Micah, Matthew, Charis & Charlotte – beginning and end, this book's for you.

Contents

III. *from* Eleventh Night

Wake Up

in memory of Seamus Heaney

A Carolina cardinal charging the study window
Woke me up to the Dundas winter
When a cat cried all night outside the big bay window

In the snow, black heart on cold white slab,
Coffin-lid thick. And I woke next morning
To the loss of the Russian Bard,

Disappearing just before the century closed.

And then today, in Hickory, seventeen years on,
Birds banged against the bedroom window
All morning long, while I lay with my boy

In the bed, resting our late-night heads.
And I woke to the loss of the Irish Bard,
And knew well what the birds had been beating out:

Wake up!
Wake up!
Wake up!

The Poet's dead!

... Yet the books will be there on the shelves, well born,
Derived from people, but also from radiance, heights.

from "And Yet The Books," by Czeslaw Milosz

I.

THE MOONGATE SONNETS

for
William 'Billy' Montgomery
(1906-1992)

The Moongate Sonnets *is dedicated to William Montgomery (1906-1992). I first met 'Billy' in the mid-1980's when I moved my family into a row of old terraced cottages in Mullaghboy, on the beautiful Islandmagee peninsula, on the north-eastern coast of Northern Ireland. (Ross Wilson inspired, I named the cottage 'Moongate'.) Having just lost his beloved wife, Grace, Billy lived on his own in the little cottage next door. Though born and bred in Belfast city, he was well-acquainted with rural Islandmagee from early childhood, and had moved there permanently following his retirement from his life-long job at Belfast's Harland & Wolff shipyard. When we met, Billy was in his late-seventies and I was in my mid-twenties, but age proved no barrier to a providential relationship. Despite the ever-present sense of loss since his passing – twenty years ago – I trust that the sonnets speak for themselves in regard to the evergreen essence of our friendship. As his loving family could no doubt better testify, Billy Montgomery was a genuinely humble, honourable, and honest Ulsterman.*

The Book of Life

He loved that moment when family members,
Long lost friends or cherished lovers,
Forgot themselves in their rush to embrace.
For him it was a foretaste of Heaven's grace.
He would hide his teary eyes by sleight-of-hand,
By channel changing and manly banter
Or by slipping to the scullery to make us supper.
He would reappear with china teacups in each hand
And create a fuss deciding which was which.
Settled, he would swear that This Is Your Life was kitsch.
Now everything has turned titanic since his death.
As I soak, foam-ruffled, in the tepid water,
Even the BE SURE deodorant bottle
Lies like a toppled king upon the shelf.

I. The First Hello

Openings and closings. Beginnings and
Endings. Windows. I first shook his cold hand
At our cottage window, one big wind night
When his ghostly face loomed at the pane, right
When it seemed our rural dream might perish.
I pushed the half window out and in he swam,
Surfacing from the darkness like a moon-
Eyed fish. *Tell me, what brought you to a place
Like this?* I leaned full forward, face to face,
And surprised myself by saying *Jesus*.
Pulling back, he studied me from tip to toe
And sighed: *Son, I'll be glad, if that's the case.*
That window, which saw the first hello, was
The window where I'd have to watch him go.

II. The Grieving Ground

Reaching the why and wherefore of the racket –
A blackbird lying by the garden gate
And her mate protesting from branch to branch –
I sensed something, turned and glanced
And caught him staring from his kitchen window.
I didn't mouth a word or make a sign,
But I knew he knew what was wrong.
He struggled round, put on a scary show,
But failed to stop the sorrow song
Or force the living from the grieving ground.
I shyly watched him shoo at grief,
Remembering the loss of his own wife,
And realised Death, the homeless thief,
Had broken in, squatted and wouldn't leave.

III. The Starlings

Breakfast dishes washed and dried, he laid his
Cobbled cassie each morning for the birds
With ground-down biscuit bits and breadcrumbs smeared
With butter, rhubarb jam and lemon curd.
In his wing-backed window seat he'd sit and sup
Until the starlings out-muscled the sparrows –
Hooligans! Greedy guts! You useless shower!
He was like a poltergeist at work,
With windows banging and blinds rattling,
As he did his best to shift those starlings.
But being cute, they just ebbed in and out
Like oil-slick waves upon the shore, which left him as –
For all his bluster, shouts and growls –
An ornithological King Canute.

IV. The Lesson

An old-fashioned stickler for hard work and routine –
Everything, inside and outside, sang pristine.
He swept the summer loanen
Until it shone like polished linoleum.
Breakfast, set the fire, radio, garden …
Days were measured to the last degree …
Lunchtime, dinnertime, paper-shop, eye-
Drops, TV, supper, then bed by ten.
All things ship-shape was the shipyard rule.
So, the time his son beaked off school
He swore that boy wouldn't act the bastard
And walked him straight back to schoolboy prison.
I wondered if it worked, if he learned his lesson.
Well, what if I told you he's now a headmaster?

V. The Groundsman

His right foot firmly planted on the square,
He crossed lines to tend the green rectangular
Of Cliftonville's Solitude stadium.
Such volunteering was a Lundy sin.
But he'd no time for the balaclava crowd,
Anonymous assassins whose faceless
Death-squads had no provable place
In a province plagued by the shroud –
Both sides were as good or as bad as the other.
Protestant Lone Ranger, it was no bother
When some cowboys blew him head-over-heel,
Out of the tunnel, onto the field,
Like a bloody, big ball of tumbleweed.
It wouldn't take long for his wounds to heal.

VI. The Cartoon Capers

The bus dropped the kids off, top of the loanen,
At the end of their little school day. They'd zoom
Round the outhouse, fly through the front door,
And dump bags on the hallway floor.
I'd greet them and hug them and smile
As they ventured to visit his wonderland –
A world full of biccies and juices, and
Goodies and baddies, with wizards and witches, *oh my!*
Sat on his settee, cushioned and comfy,
They'd gaze goggle-eyed at TV.
He'd serve them, then sneak out and play
On our window to posse me round for a peek.
We'd clown and we'd caper and mimic
Their features – till they'd rise up and chase us away.

VII. The Eyewitness

Just six years of age, he was eyewitness
To the first voyage of the world's greatest
Ship. It was so huge it made his heart laugh
To watch it fill the window of the Lough:
From city to sea, from sea to sky,
Full of man's invulnerable majesty.
Now we all know, as it transpired, that they
Were full of infallible fantasy.
Among them be it, I can hear him say –
So much for man's invulnerability.
But then I picture him as a boy,
Lying window-eyed on the watching cliff,
Unable to fathom, there in mid-wave,
That ship going down like a faulty toy.

VIII. The Yardman

Stowed away safely in a box upstairs
(For fear we'd feel he'd put on airs),
The man who didn't even own a car,
Owned a letter signed, 'Elizabeth R.'
She'd sealed his British Empire Medal
For services to shipping at Harland & Wolff.
Though proud, he required no Royal proof
Of his place in the Belfast shipyard's tidal
Crews. Nicknamed 'The Whippet' for laddering
Speed – boiler-room, top deck, to the quay –
The gifted souvenir considered savvy
Was David Hammond's 'The Boat Factory'.
His 'John Hancock' proved fit for friends to see:
'For Billy, who knows it all. Best, Davy.'

IX. The Back Garden

Sweat falling from his brow onto cold clay,
He turned the earth at the end of the day.
Townie, with appetite for country work,
He used the spade and graipe like knife and fork.
Upending moist heads of Medusa loam,
He finger-sieved fat garden worms and weeds
That had made a mess of his perfect beds,
Stripping them like snakes from a gorgon's comb.
My kids were dumbstruck – both mouths wide open –
As he hung worms from the cherry blossom.
When evening fell, I would call out their names –
He'd point their hiding place without one word,
Then plant his spade like a battlefield sword,
And watch the dying sun go down in flames.

X. The Last Look

Feeling his heart's battery running down,
He took me with him for a dander round
The fields to see his childhood home again.
We stood in sad ruins in soft Irish rain
With two dappled stallions who watched us scan
Newspapers that lined the walls and conjured
Up bloody ghosts of the dead and injured
From two World Wars. The horses had moved in.
We pottered homeward by the sandy street
Where waves dropped pearly bracelets at his feet,
And on the Gobbins headland ridge-trees shot
Back weathered wind-swept branches in salute.
We turned away – but not before his hot
Eyes had set longingly on one last look.

XI. The Loved Ephemeral

I cried my eyes out at the funeral –
Earthbound tears for the loved ephemeral –
Sitting near the rear of the congregation,
Unable to match their restraint of emotion:
That Ulster Presbyterian virtue,
Fostered from cradle to grave,
By people who'd flourish backhanded waves
At the playing of heartstrings in public view.
Some sneaked looks at me over their shoulder,
The old were subtle, the younger bolder.
Imagine what they would have thought
If those tsunami tears had built and built,
Lifting his coffin from its catafalque
And carrying it homeward up Belfast Lough.

XII. The Dream of Goodbye

In the dream world, he said goodbye for good.
It played itself out like a rehearsal would –
The knock at the door, the hurry round,
The dreadful heartsick fear of what we'd find.
We found him dead upon his flooring,
Beside his bed, the faintest photocopy
Of himself, an image from Fellini,
Not lying really, more like hovering.
When the neighbour went downstairs to phone,
She left us, momentarily, on our own,
Dreamtime still. Then my heart began to hum
As he opened his eyes, opened his mouth,
And from our loosened tongues the truth
Eased out: *I love you, Billy*; and, *I love you, son*.

XIII. The Changeful Tap

The water would suddenly thin to a trickle,
Some summer evenings while filling the kettle –
It took an eternity just to make tea.
And I'd know with an absolute certainty
He'd made his way back to the garden
To toddle around the immaculate rows,
To sprinkle the heads of infant flowers
From the font of his watering can.
It was such chores that kept him happy.
Still, I'd secretly curse our shared supply
And covet the moment when I'd have control.
But nowadays reaching to turn on the tap,
I sometimes fall for the futile hope
The running water might suddenly slow.

XIV. The Ghosts Remain

How sadly once familiar things seem strange –
How much changes for the worse, in our eyes,
Of the homes we love and leave. It's as if
This is the only way to cope with why we left:
Returning to find them neglected or
Re-arranged; not surviving all that well
Without us. It means that we can tell
Ourselves how blessed we definitely are
To have left them trailing in our wake,
Sailing off for Elsewhere, waltzing with Fate.
But then, ghosts of ourselves and of old friends
Surface round us, smiling gently – they know
That our indifference is mostly show:
And know they will be with us when it ends.

Epilogue
The Double Crown

Sometimes I feel like I let you down in
The end, old friend, spending time out running
Around with other best friends. I guess I
Never learned from the late neglect of my
Lonely grandmother. Funny, last word I
Shared with her over the phone was *Jesus*.
Just in case I'm right – if I let us
Down in life – I hope you'll accept poetry
In the hereafter as poor recompense
From the man you mentored who's seen some sense.
So take this double crown (wreathed at each end)
And you wear yours, and I'll wear mine
And let's break bread together across space and time:
Me, in the here-now; you, in the there-then.

II.

HICKORY STATION

For here, as nowhere else on earth,
Men were brought together for a moment
At the beginning or end
Of their innumerable journeys,
Here one saw their greetings and farewells,
Here, in a single instant,
One got the entire picture of the human destiny.
Men came and went, they passed and vanished,
And all were moving through the moments of their
lives
To death,
All made small tickings in the sound of time –

– from "The Railroad Station" by Thomas Wolfe

The Recovery

for JB & AM

The bed had become his whole home.
Then one morning, late, he pulled back

The covers, like he was opening a garden gate,
Strode across the lawn-lush carpet to the veranda

Of his desk, sat down, took up his pen,
And sent it sailing on the ocean page.

Mortal

for PAC

A goddess in the corner of Crescent Moon Café,
Who has given us this evening a stellar display

Of feminine fire worthy of first Adam alone,
Is now holding the cold candle of her new iPhone,

And by cellular floodlight we can suddenly trace
The ordinary lineaments of her mortal face.

Whale

Waiting for my students to gather,
I was silently lamenting how
Blue whales can't hear each other

Sing, as they were once able
To do, freely, from ocean to ocean
Across our watery globe

'Cause we've drowned the seven seas
In an incessant babble,
When a student cruised into class

With a cell shell held to her ear.
When I casually asked if she'd tell us
Who she was speaking to, her

Eyebrows lifted and her face flushed
As she pointed to another girl
Sitting with her back to the wall, and gushed,

Her! We all smiled. But I knew well,
That class was going to hear the tale
'Failing Songs of the Great Blue Whale.'

Among the Lavender

Honeybees spend their busy day
Hovering among the lavender
With constant co-workers for company.

Each a natural-born spacewalker,
They lend the light leaves some sway
As they drift from flower to flower.

For them, perhaps, the pale purple
Of the holy herb is just
Another colour, and the beautiful

Fragrance may be only a wind-blown
Aroma-sugar aimed solely at us,
But from sunup to sundown

Honeybees love lavender and toil together
For the good of the whole hive.
Come dailigone, a few workaholics are

Left drone-dozy on a psychedelic buzz,
Dream-heavy with sweet nectamares
On their soft perfumy beds.

What the hive finally harvests,
The lavender won't miss.
Lavender exists for this.

Blackout

for Molly

Everything's an icicle out-of-doors,
Coated with the cold, clear killer.
It works away at tree limbs,
A wet suffocation,
Holds them in frozenness until they drown,
Give up the ghost,
Crack and fall to the snow ground.

Power lines have similarly fallen,
Turning the whole town off.
Outside, the moon's odd oval
Is the only light left on.
Inside, we nod to goodness
For candles and beer and bread.
We read by flickers from a screen of little flames,

Sharing Milosz's last masterpiece, **Second Space**,
Ourselves in a kind of forgotten second space.
O world without artificial light,
Without the microchip or the microwave,
Without the fast food language of the television set,
Take our thanks, page after page, for being lit-up and well-fed
By the wisdom words of one man's bright old age.

Madam Moon

The strip of light
under the study door
made me think

my desk lamp was burning.
But when I rose
to take a look,

I found that it was glory
from a full, low moon,
holding court

in the clear Carolina sky.
Behind her regal smile
moon hid a hint of hurt,

seeing I'd mistook
her for a little light bulb
or a common crook.

Thieves Like Us

Well into evening, we crossed into Estrie, Quebec's bucolic land of Victorian mansions, where Mary's a fountain and Jesus a garden gnome. We'd driven north from Thoreau's Concord, up through wooded Vermont and Maine, following the trail of rich Confederates who – lowering their blinds as they passed through New England – trundled the rails in private coaches for summering free of white hot weather and 'dastardly Yankees'.

We left the main road at sleepy Barnston, veered over to the verge of a farmer's field and silenced the car. Peering past the black-and-white mapped sides of curious cattle, we were struck by an unusual outhouse, a round barn, a thing we had heard of but never seen. Built with wafer-thin window slits and nipple-topped, as if bell-belfried, it was an unearthly marriage of mosque and Martello tower. Its roundness arose from the local belief that the Devil hides in corners – one more strange version of voodoo, since the book has him prince of this globular world and the sightless seer of paradise has written that Heaven is square. After she took the holiday snap, we chit-chatted, until I murmured that our hearts mustn't be round. After that, nothing more seemed sayable.

Slowly we became aware of a low ringing, the gentle tambourine jingle of the cicada, and then, lifting our eyes, we feasted on the eucharist of the full moon that blazed over everything, doing its best to salve the soul. Refreshed, I fired the ignition, and, as she held my free hand in hers, we pressed on, steering for Kingston, halfway on our journey home.

The Dead Bride

for Geoffrey Hill

In far-off Carolina,
On the roadside turret
Of our evening porch,

I found this poem
When I instinctively
Lifted your open book

And clapped it shut
To trap
A dithery mosquito.

When I re-opened the paper tomb,
There he was,
The dark suitor,

Pinned back
Against the thin sheet,
Full blood bags

Unbelievably spilled
Across
The predestined verse:

'So white I was, he would have me cry
Unclean! Murderously
To heal me with far-fetched blood.'

Boxing Day

I was greeted by the loud crying of birds.
I looked out across the neighbour's yard
To a bare tree, perfectly decorated with blue jays,

Each one a blue bulb in the late afternoon.
I'd never seen so many bluejays at one time.
My eyes then dropped onto a bed of fallen

Leaves, onto a hawk that was riding
On top of a luckless blue jay, whose plumage
Had no doubt marked it as a certainty;

No aerial aggressor need have wasted tricks
On such brilliant blue on green.
I could tell that the hawk was having its

Way with the floored bird, and it was disturbingly
Sexual how the hawk handled its prey – clapping
Its wings, gently, to keep it in place; casually coaxing

The dying bird to behave itself at the dining table;
Expertly tightening its grip to have its food
While things were hot and fresh. My own blood

Rose, powerless, one fenced garden away, witnessing
Weakly what looked like purely malevolent lust.
I shouted, of course, and made loud growling

Sounds and shouts to make the hawk stop; go away.
And was thinking of 'Boxing Day', of how that many birds
Could beat up on the brute blood and save the day …

But just then, the whole tree-full of them ceased
Crying and took off – right before the hawk had had enough.
Doubtless, no other blue jay would have wanted to be next …

Or did their grief only last as long as the feathery feast?

from
Texts

for Alan Mearns

Just sieving the daily dust, panning for poems ...
Sent

Last night, the whole forest
moved and shook itself
like a huge drenched dog.
Sent

... all night, skin-tight, hold-warm,
sheet-surf rippling and rolling
towards the coasts of love ...
Sent

Rising and falling on the chest-swells,
our wee one sleeps on love-liners, human oceans.
Sent

Too tired to deal with the fuss,
we've let the bairn bed down
in the valley of himself
between the two mountains of us.
Sent

I love those late night
living room light bulbs,
those insomnia suns.
Sent

It doesn't matter how vast it is 'out there'.
We all know the 'in here' is vaster.
Sent

It's dark, but what's 'missing' in the Universe
truly matters ... works just as well
for what's left out of one good verse.
Sent

Does everything earthly also yearn to go off with a bang?
Sent

From the darkling porch on rainy nights,
I watch cars photocopying the glassy streets.
Sent

Somewhere between Pound and Williams,
nearly every thing is 'like a',
… things are seldom what they are.
Sent

I said, *Poetry? Poetry?*
Poetry is verbal mathematics,
the algebra of the soul! Then fled.
Sent

What we deeply believe is right today
is often deeply wrong tomorrow –
the shifting sands of scientific inquiry …
Sent

An instant after they strike ground,
each raindrop wears a rainy crown.
Sent

Good poets are ventriloquists
And ev'ry dummy fits their fists.
Sent

One can only pour so much love into a word …
but everything that's left out, survives, unheard.
Sent

Poetry's tough. It won't let you bully
folk into liking it. It's all about love.
Sent

Everything's a preparation for separation.
Sent

Fidelity to poetry is such a healthy madness ...

The Clock Flower

As far as the rest of the universe is concerned,
Maybe we're like the feather-fluff of the clock flower,

The ghostly snow-sphere of the dying dandelion
That the child holds up in wide-eyed wonder,

Which the mother says to blow on to tell the time
By how many breath-blows it takes before the airy seed

All flies away, leaving her child clutching a bare stem.
And where our humanness might go, who knows?

And when it lands – takes root – what grows?

Matter

for Damian Gorman

tracing the skeleton
under the skin tonight,

I am amazed,
I am, again, to feel that

we're all just matter ...
who nevertheless sense,

deep down,
that we really matter

Cardboard

Last night, while leisurely reading on the toilet,
I became aware of a strange heat against my bare right
Leg, caused by the cardboard side of a huge Huggies

Diaper box, emblazoned with the promise, Snug and Dry.
I immediately thought of people living in cardboard cities;
Of just how grateful one could be for cardboard warmth.

I was re-reading Wordsworth's 'Tintern Abbey',
About the *still, sad music of humanity,*
About its *ample power / to chasten and subdue.*

When I finished, and washed my hands, and brushed my teeth,
A small quiet voice seemed to almost audibly say –
Face it; life's only ever really good, if it's good for you.

Ever Émigrés

Always breath-taking when kings of the passerines
Begin to gather on local telegraph wires,
Slick squadrons somersaulting into lines

For their autumnal assault on the south.
Easy to cast them as crochets and quavers,
But the two-fisted wind-grip of Ulster's north-

East makes them swivel like foosball figures
As they rev up for take-off for Africa.
Like us Irish, swallows and books are ever émigrés,

And I imagine my own book-flock lining up in Belfast
Mist for their trans-Atlantic flight to America.
Not all make it, though thousands do, returning to roost

In western nests, under familiar wooden eaves.
As I spread their paper wings, strum folio feathers,
The heart sings and soars over the mind's dark seas.

Defriended

for ASM

(after Auden)

Lazily screening late last night it caught my eye
That we had ninety mutual Facebook friends,
Though tonight I notice we've only eighty-nine.

I'm betting that someone grew properly weary
Of yours truly's postings in the poetry games,
And acted decisively on pull-the-plug time.

But supposing that we shoulder blame equally,
Brother-bound in arenas of sharable shames,
Affection says – let the defriended tag be mine.

Bad Day for the Nihilist

To be perfectly honest, it was a bad day for the nihilist.
But just how could I have known that when
I finished up administering the final exam
at the community college, and stood waiting wist-

fully on the starlit kerb for my wife to come my way,
that Wal-Mart would prove to be such a temple
of revelation? We normally just go there for some ample
groceries – though we did call them 'messages' back in the day.

So as we wandered aimlessly around the thankfully
vacant aisles in search of nothing in particular,
just picking up a few staples as we went, as we are
wont to do, we were suddenly met by a balloon that randomly

ballooned out in front of us, and floated upwards,
seemingly unnoticed by any others. My dear wife caught it,
but just as quickly let it go. Then I guldered, *Catch it!*
and leapt up and grabbed it. Still laughing, my wife wondered

what was printed on it. *Only 'Welcome Baby*, I said.
Well, we looked at each other, and smiled, and sang in sync,
Noooo waaaaay!!!! But just before we left the shopping rink
we exchanged looks with each other again and decided

that maybe we should take (two) tests home. And yes, we passed
them both. Now, every time I tell the story, a listener will say,
That story is sending shivers up my spine! And I will always reply:
Let me tell you – those shivers up your spine? They were mine, first.

St Francis and the Kisses

Leaves from the Japanese maple have perished,
Some dry-scrunched, some burgundy-powdered,
Deep pink-pastel resin dusting the dainty feet
Of our garden genie, hooded, head-bent, Crossed.
Cold contemplative, bird-lover, folds of his stone robes
Garden-algaed, in gentle green-greyed waves
Rolling round him, he's reminiscent of a Zeppelin
Cover or an elfin enchanter from a famous fiction.

My youngest always makes his way over to him,
Bends down and looks him in the eye, smiling,
Puts an arm around his shoulders, kisses him on his crown.
Though I knew that this would likely end up in a poem,
It was waiting for its mirror in my older son,
Bending over me in front of the stereo station,
Blessing me – in my head-down, cupped-chin slumber
Before slipping to his holiday bed – with a kiss I remember.

Behind the Lines

My boy sits in his red plastic sand pit
As happy as a baby at the beach.
I help him spoon sand into his bucket,

Trusting that our redneck, beachless summers
Don't offend our nice suburban neighbours,
When a baby Cardinal drop-clatters

Through the thick branches of a garden tree,
Like a paratrooper gone well astray
Behind the lines of a bitter enemy.

The father flit-frets in a nearby hedge,
But tufty-head quickly finds both his feet
And his wonderful wings and flies offstage

To rendezvous with his feathered platoon.
I'm booking a front row seat to watch them
Strut their aerial stuff some evening soon.

Kingdom

Unable to make time to mow the luscious lawn,
I find it has been taken by a host of honeysuckle
Armed with big blades and spears, fireflies moving

Diligently above them, pulsing prayerful novas
In benedictory sway, shedding their golden-green
Blessings before battle. The honeysuckle soldiers

Have already conquered the garden; side of the street.
Seems they are massing, come nightfall, to advance.
Before I wake, their kingdom could be complete.

As They Go

It's hard to imagine me saying so,

But I am sad to see the first fireflies
This evening, for I know they signal that
Darkness is on its rounds. They never lie.

It is as if their miraculous lights
Are the encore excess of our bright star;
Bonus tracks to ease us into the night's

Final curtain fall, on yet another
Worldly show. They work their way up from earth
Through trees, to the heavens, from birth to death

(Or perhaps it's death to birth) as they go.

Planted

We have no prairies
To slice a big sun at evening
            —Seamus Heaney, 'Bogland'

I
We have no porches to share a slice of melon on back home,
To sit on to watch the sun go down, least not where I come from:
No tree frogs, no cicadas, no rhythmic rattling in treetops.
Closest we come to them are the squeaky brakes of passing cars,
Or the sing-song goings-on of late evening's emptying bars.
And no fireflies. Lightning bugs. Blinking on and off like sudden
Thoughts. Nearest we come to them is on soggy, foggy nights when
Unmanned, landlocked lighthouses attempt to keep us off the rocks.

II
Planted here, though, enjoying the electrons of evening,
I can picture certain characters from home as they lean
Against door lintels, or perch on front-step chairs and look out,
Or gather on public benches on the outskirts of town
To swap stories, then silently stare at thinning traffic,
Well past sundown, under the scrubbed spud of a summer moon.
I probably share some genes with such curbside Calvinists,
Happy to sit and watch as heat waves shiver into mist.

One to Another

for Lori & Clay Templeton

Found sitting a Carolina spell, thinking how
We're either building up or bringing down,
When my neighbour from across the way

Raises his hand and shares a wordless wave.
I raise mine silently and bounce it back,
Happy to feel the force of his friendly move,

That costs us nothing when we give it up:
The kind of exchange I used to have
With Ulster country people as they sat

Upon their trundling tractors on rural roads
Or closed their gates on cattle fields,
Repaying urban patience with a hand and nod.

It's good to put our hands up in this way,
To see ourselves simply mirrored in another,
As naturally as one wave will make its way

From one unforgotten seashore to another.

Q&A

for Woody Trathen

Native Americans
Built no castles?

The many mountains
Were their castles.

And the teepee
That they settled for?

That was the
Mountain metaphor.

Hotel Nature

I've never fully noticed until this evening
How loudly birds chitter-chatter before bed.
Such bird babble! Such tower of song!

Too tired to google away my ignorance,
I wonder if it's simply an inter-flock
Roll-call of present and corrects;

Nest-calls of Goodnight, John-boys;
Plethora's of passionate sweet nothings?
Incredible, how it all abruptly stops.

Though there are always some random tweets,
Some feathery heartthanks, dusky prayers.
Tonight, given my mood, it's appropriate

To imagine them coming from the tittery
Back row of a touring bird chorus –
Some raffish, humourous, banter-boy's silly

Craic before Hotel Nature's final lights out.

Mosquito

for Ian Duhig

Ian, in the kingdom of porch,
when natural light dims, we Irish are huge human
blood banks fit for the robbing.

As you can imagine, it's never good
when the super-saver citronella candle, wax-shaped to
the big black metal bucket, goes suddenly out;

when that pope-hatted-flame has burnt
an almighty hole through the candle-heart down
to the bare bucket base.

So I rush in and out, take
a sharp kitchen knife to the plentiful side slabs
and watch them crumble

inwards as easily as Arctic ice.
A flaring flame greets, once again, the grateful wick.
Relatively unbitten, thinking of you,

I put my head religiously back in the books.

Redbreast

Memorial Day. Mown grass. Wee man down for doze.
I'm sitting on the evening porch; it's humid, but nice.
A rising breeze riffles my magazines like flags.

Only garden drama centres on the new-born robin
Who couldn't be more obviously trusting, more exposed,
Caught out in the open, perched on the low garden

Wall. Clearly not a flier, yet. I'm busily distracting
The feline who shares our porch, in hope that the fledgling
Can quickly find its wings. The parents are crisscrossing

Anxiously overhead, sounding their alarms, shouting
Support from the safety of trees. Wonderful to think
That the last thing little redbreast has to fear at this time,

Surrounded by all natural perils – the unfriendly blood
Of the air; toying cat claws on the ground – is human.
I raise my brimming glass in thankfulness and drain it good.

Leaves

Under the thinning canopy of autumn trees,
I watch over my son while he plays in the leaves.

His blossoming boyhood is a blessing to see,
In the light of those leaves which are falling from me.

The Rocking Tree

for RC and The Riddle Ring

When the wind shear swelled
With Vincent panache,

I felt for nestlings
In the rocking tree,

And made them a wish
That they'd weather well,

Like sober sailors
On a drunken sea.

Beseech

for Seth Collings Hawkins

Dangerous to entrust the grains of truth
To the hourglass hands of us humans.
I am verily heartsick of party politics,
Of constitutional charades, and so-called
Social posts from our puritanical patriots
Or baby-boomers flirting with pat-riots –

The positively right telling the other
That they're so black-and-whitely wrong.
I have seen it, and I've heard it all before,
And sadly not in another lifetime.
I sympathise with those who know that money
Talks, and that it stinks, and that the love of it

Is a hothouse for the flowers of evil.
I'm with those who know that simply holding on
Is all that they've got, or are ever likely to get,
And that faithful letting go is their only holding on.
And I remember the great dissenter, John Hewitt,
Cleverly quoting Cromwell – demonic to Catholics –

In an interview with Dublin's *Irish Times*,
Referencing his exhortation to the Presbyterians
Of Scotland: "I beseech you in the bowels of Christ
Think it possible you may be mistaken."
If even Cromwell could conceive of the second guess,
Isn't it about time that we all did the same?

The Falls

It's still hard to fathom
the man who backstroked
his way over Niagara Falls.

What was he thinking?
What had crossed/was crossing
his mind as he water-wheeled

himself to the barbarous brink?
There have been loonies,
of course, who have willingly

dared the Falls in homemade
barrels; and there have even
been times when we ourselves have

slipped in under the suicide's skin
(before such thoughts have become
a self-pitying offence to them),

but to just seemingly, serenely,
backstroke over the lethal lip,
with each steady stroke signalling

a confident, torpedoing,
full-handed farewell to life?
Now that's another kind of unbeing.

Local newspapers concurred
that it would take some time
for the body to surface. If ever.

For All Is There

Surf City, NC, Summer 2013

As the old full moon succumbs to cloud,
leaving a nicotine stain in its shroud,
I lift my glassy eyes to the sound shore,
where every light's a Ferris-wheel or clock flower.

Up this high, ear-level with tree frogs and cicadas,
I have never heard them so interrupt thought.
Hickory-porched, they're only a background comfort,
no louder than those childhood pull-back drags

we would rev and race across the scullery floor.
Old Horace said that no poems worth their
salt were ever written by drinkers of water.
Sounds like a Bukowski bite, a faithful follower

of the blushful glass … and just as soon
as now, clamorous clouds close the sky dome,
and bolt lightning turns the lightless wetland
into a floodlit field, sending any stranded

sinners onto their hopeful hands and knees.
But from this balcony tonight, I could happily
drama-fall into the hands and arms of the electric air
and fully trust the unseen. For all is there.

Lent

Few things as eye-soothing as dying light
From fall's show, temporally on loan.
The trees that line the avenue tonight
Have lost the many colours they have worn
With such dapper-dazzle during the day.
The sun, wardrobe manager of daytime,
Is the robber who has left them poorly
Dressed in the post-show monochrome evening.
The waning moon, lunula of lent light,
One half lit, the other blackened by night,
Portrays this substance and shadow of life,
And simply *is*, in sunshine and in shade.
While we swing wildly from singing to strife,
Forgetful that we're similarly made.

A Dark Leaf

for Ross Wilson

Along the alley of our avenue,
Birds flicker nervously between tall trees,
Nests bobbing under the black-and-blue
Of a stormful sky. The high branch-kelp sways
In the lifting wind-wave, delivering
A dark leaf through the mailbox of my porch,
Dropping onto my notebook, like a sign.
Everything is darkening. Lightning flirts
With telegraph poles. Thunder-balls rumble
The bowling lanes overhead, their mumble
Silencing the cooing of a dove.
Here comes the rain, so redolent of home.
Odd, the things we miss of the things we love.
Time to pack up and go inside, alone.

Just Enough

for Angela Beaver Simmons

Who knows what my neighbour's kitchen holds
Of love or loss, of longing or loneliness,

Or of any clichéd combination of the above.
But as the darkness draws itself down,

Light burns across the kitchen borders
Onto the window-high azaleas

In sufficient excess to flame the flowery
Promise just enough to catch my weary eye,

To resurrect my buried thankfulness,
To rekindle my own love affair with desire.

So I Wish

Matthew, my oldest
son's a proper poet
now, something that
seems incredible
somehow, though I
should have known
that when he published
a poem of mine
upon his ribs
that poetry had
announced itself
in residence
beneath the skin.

Then I come
into the room,
just now, to find
Micah, my youngest,
squatting on the floor
beside his drawing pad.
He has become bored
with the paper page
and has turned
the inky pen upon himself:
arms, legs, feet, toes –
the freehand abandon
of toddler tattoos.

And then I recall
that the Father's laws
are written not upon
the page nor on the skin
but deeper down,
within, in ink
the colour of

our deepest sin, in
heart-red that rolls round
the veins, seals the soul,
and so I wish my sons both
poetry, art, and the Word
that makes them whole.

Neighbourhood

I dwell in a neighbourhood where most driveways
are laid with white marble stones of a kind which
are normally raked over posh people's graves

and where the house opposite is a dead ringer for
the only home I could ever draw easily at school –
roofed square, four windows, winding pathway to door –

and where the green grassy garden is treated to a trim
never having been left long enough to merit a cut
and where I can sit on my porch and read and dream

and sip chilled wine for hours on end while tree frogs
and cicadas blend their comforting evening fugue
and the only thing to fear is the mighty mosquito …

what a change from the streets of my Rathcoole childhood
when if I stood at our door and simply gazed out
I'd be greeted with, *who the fuck are you lookin' at?*

III.

from
ELEVENTH NIGHT

for
Martin Beattie

NHOJ

I'm big McClatchy and I don't give a fuck,
Except for your bird if she's fit for a buck.
I tattooed my own name on my forehead once
– Just actin' the lig, like, playin' the dunce –
It was a wee homemade job, done at the house,
And I managed to screw up my own name – twice.
When I finally nailed it, it looked fuckin' well,
Except for the fact it was so hard to tell
('Cause it looked more like some stupid fenian scrawl)
If it was written in proper English at all.
So I asked my mates for their opinion
And was pissed off to see them all fall about laughin'.
But they did let me know that I'd got it wrong –
Instead of 'JOHN', it really read 'NHOJ'.
You can imagine my fuckin' horror ...
Though it taught me never to trust in the mirror.

I. Bones and Blood

My bones are pavement, and my blood cement,
I'm the Protestant half of an Irish lament.
From the Rathcoole housing estate, I'm torn,
By way of Dromara and the Mountains of Mourne.
    Within one-nine-six, on Derrycoole Way,
I made my memories, and remember the day
That a workman left footprints forevermore
Upon the unset pathway to our front door;
Footprints I knew would be someone's undoing
If they were not watching where they were going:
Sunk down in cement by some Immanent Will
For my brother, Annesley, who was nearly killed
When he went for a trip, and had a great fall,
Headfirst through the glass door and into our hall,
Because he was basically being a get
To beat me to money to buy a *Seajet*.
Being hard on his heels, I witnessed it all –
Saw him bloodied, lifeless, and flat on the floor,
Face-shrouded in the lace curtain that adorned
Our front door. But you could never keep him down
And out; he was soon up and washed and away –
Good prep for a boy who would face the IRA.
    Much stranger than fiction, the funniest thing
Was that our family had been preparing
For days for something similar to happen
To me, set down in stone by a prediction
Made by my Presbyterian grandmother,
Who would work herself up into a lather
Because of her unfortunate psychic powers
That would often keep her awake for long hours
Worrying about the poor apparitions
From her vivid, dream-given revelations.
    Although she couldn't say when or where or why,
My granny foresaw airplanes fall from the sky,
And prophesied the time when a spoil-tip slipped down

To stop up young mouths in a coal mining town.
She said she had dreamt that an ominous cloud
Grew bigger and darker and covered a crowd
Of innocent children sat in a room
And brought them black rain from the kingdom of doom …
She swore they were singing a beautiful hymn
With voices like birds warbling sweetly in whin.
The Aberfan disaster would strike home each year
When Welsh male voice choirs would bring down a tear.
    But as sure as such dreams, every prediction
Would be fulfilled with a different victim
Suffering the bad (never good) of any
Dream scenario phoned through by my granny
To a daughter, son or other relation –
I had been earmarked for Annesley's misfortune.

II. The Deep Field

Blurry Christmas tree lights in the corner gloom
Become the Hubble deep field, making this room
A portal through which I travel back in time
To seek out the company of my own kind.
    Early Christmas Eve; my young brother and I
Are already in bed, the only night my
Parents knew we'd volunteer to climb the stairs
Without the need for either of their orders.
I'm the oldest by three whole years, coming ten,
Old enough to know the saddest truth by then:
That Santa Claus is just a storybook sham,
Another figment of human invention.
But I was predestined to be a friend of
The imagination; found myself in love
With things invisible to sense and to plain
Sight – had reinvented him; believed again.
    I haven't yet moved into the box room. I'm
Still sharing a bedroom, glad that at bedtime
I can safely ask that the landing light be
Left on and blame it on my brother, as he
Still has an excuse for not liking the dark.
Asking is no problem when dad is at work.
But tonight, I know that my dad's Santa Claus,
And my about-to-burst heart's primed with applause.
    Lying beside my brother in semi-gloom,
I can hear sounds rising from the living room:
Comforting parental happy talk and low
Canned laughter from a comedy Christmas show
Everyone liked – the great Morecambe and Wise ...
Though my brother gets beaten by sleep, my eyes
Are set firmly on the prize of Christmas morn.
I know we can't get up until after dawn,
But the very second that daylight comes round,
We both race downstairs without touching the ground.
    Though working class kids, not mammon anointed,

I can honestly say we aren't disappointed:
We get toy soldiers, and football boots, and kits,
Cool games, and annuals, and even two bikes.
Our mum and dad rise to look at our faces,
Then head back to bed to resume their places
In a dream world that we wouldn't begrudge them,
Since they've left us in our version of heaven.
  Before the long day's out, before bed seems good,
We turn our attention to kids' Christmas food:
Not turkey and stuffing with gravy and peas,
But from padding presents left under the tree –
Selection boxes created perfectly,
Full of Mars Bars, Milky Ways and Galaxys.

III. The Grey Van

It always appears in Innis Avenue,
So, from Derrycoole Way, it's hidden from view,
But the long, community-friendly, horn-toot
Sounds its arrival, and we're begging for loot
To saunter round the corner to join children
Already in a line for *the* ice-cream man.
No need for a Mr. Softy or Whippy
Breakneck sprint, fearful that he'll have gone away
Before we'll reach him, because he's patient, seems
A genuine gentleman, not an ice-cream
Cowboy, arriving to the redneck 'Dixie',
Anywhere, and at anytime of the day
Or night, blasting out the Southern anthem from
A multi-coloured, plastic-cone-topped wagon.
Don't get me wrong, it's part of our pantheon;
Just looks like a tasteless giant's novelty crown,
While the ice-cream man's van is synonymous
With a kind of understated ice-cream class.
His small, smoke-grey Morris Minor Mini-Van,
Immaculately kept, showroom condition,
Rolls to kerbside standstill like a welcome hearse
Or a taxi on time for a tipper's purse.
No need for lettering; a marketer's dream:
Miniature, working-class Rolls-Royce of ice-cream.
Although he's no undertaker – more like The
Slider Provider, The Ice-Cream Supremo, The
Neapolitan Magician, The King of
The Poke – he has a quiet, certain something of
The undertaker's reserved, stoic manner,
And a gentle grandfatherly demeanour.
And there's always something about his clean-cut
Image, his light jacket over proper shirt
And tie, that lends him a double-life aura –
Like he's a doctor by day, chemist or a
Surgeon or a dentist or big shot lawyer ...

But by night – Master-Butcher of Vanilla!
He turns towards us from the driver's side and takes
Our window orders for sliders, crisps, cones, flakes,
For our fathers' cigarettes, whose cellophane-
Slickness somehow seems risqué coming from him.
And what's between is his work board and money
Tray, where coins are sifted and sorted, money
Stamped with kings and queens, and the Poet's horses
And hens, hounds, salmon, pigs, bulls and hares …
By his leg, low down's another money bag,
Which holds the lighter currency of our swag.
But it's when he reaches back for a new block
Of cartoned delight that a Bowie's knife-knack
Deftly kicks in, as he open-ends' the cartons,
Slicing ice-cream into perfect portions,
And presents them, always, with the grace of old-
Fashioned, unfussed, professional *quid pro quo.*

    Before I let it go, what I remember
Most fondly is the drizzly Ulster weather
Late Sunday afternoons and evenings when I
Am the solitary client at kerbside.
I have the grey van and the ice-cream man all
To myself. He often rewards his loyal
Customers with something a bit cheaper, or
Free, waiving the search for the extra copper.
What passes wordless between us, now, is lovely,
Worth more than money. And lives, in memory.

IV. Spot the Ball

At last, after the headlines have been scoured,
After the death notices have been devoured,
With *ah, that's terrible* or *such a young age*,
The 'Tele' reaches me, folded at the page
I've been waiting on, with blue ballpoint in hand,
Ready to lend my young football brain to land
A welcome windfall by winning 'Spot The Ball':
It's a photograph from a local football
Match, players bucklepping all over the place,
Epitome of focus on ev'ry face,
Just enough to persuade that they know the way
To the ball that has been airbrushed from the fray,
The ghost ball that if you pinpoint with an 'X'
Will let your family sit back and relax.
I don't know that a biroed cross will never
Be fairly acknowledged by money-makers,
And so all my attempts to target the ball,
With hindsight, are much less than no chance at all.
That doesn't stop me, now, from doing my best
To conjure the impossible jackpot 'X'.
Then an uncle leans over and interjects,
Sure, never mind the ball – get on with the match!
Another joins in with more uncle banter,
An Irish League game? Ball could be anywhere!
All less than nothing to my concentration,
Aided by mother's motherly protection,
Give over you pair, our Adrian's inspired,
And you'll not be laughing when we've all retired!
I'm in the zone, in my grandparents' living
Room and, despite the odds, I'm more than hoping
That a solitary 'X' will hit the spot.
Secretly, even I know that it will not.
But why not? Why not? Why shouldn't it be so?
Answer's from them that signed 'X', not long ago.

V. Lissue

I stand in tears in the alien playground,
Watching my mother sailing away around
The bend in the front seat of an ambulance.
I'm left at Lissue House for convalescence.
Post-op children are sent here to get well
From the Royal Victoria Hospital.
Although shell-shocked, forsaken, I understand
My mother's reason for fibbing, to pretend
She was only going to talk to someone
For a minute – her way of getting back home
With her worry-weary heart almost intact.
It'll be days before she'll be allowed back
For a first visit. Such knowledge is feeding fears
When a voice from behind me says, *Dry your tears*
Mate, it's OK, you'll live to fight another
Day. Welcome to 'The Zoo'! It's flippin' cracker!
Still gripping the wire fencing that keeps us in,
I swivel round to study the form of him
Who speaks. He has the wild look of someone who's
A bit cream-crackers, not all here, few loose screws,
But I'm glad of some comfort in this new place,
Even from a stranger with a strangeful face.
He's Ivor, 'Big Ivor', with a weight issue,
And he takes me on my first tour round Lissue.
  To a wee boy that's used to terraced Rathcoole,
Lissue is a haunted house from Scooby Doo,
With a hint of St. Trinian's thrown into
The mix – not only boys' dorms, but girls' dorms, too.
The dorms are really just big communal halls
Lined with hospital beds down their long side walls.
Big Ivor's delighted that the new boy – me –
Will bed down beside him, providentially.
There's just enough room between beds for lockers
With cupboards friendly to Lucozade bottles.
Dorm side we're facing has towering high windows,

Shuttered, come night, to slay countryside shadows.
At one end of the hall, high up on the wall,
Is a TV set mounted to serve us all.
    But before I get to properly settle,
I'm summoned to test my masculine mettle
By two young nurses who are doing their best
To lighten the trauma which I have to face.
Since my kidney treatment back at the Royal,
I've endured a urination ritual
Involving many small humiliations
Necessary to ease my urinary pains.
When I pee, it's bloody, and it feels, at best,
Like I'm peeing hot liquefied broken glass.
So pre-pee, from the waist on down, I'm clabbered
In Vaseline, then taken to a prepared
Bath of scalding water, which I will sit in
While going, the shock of the heat confusing
The brain into thinking there's no pain peeing.
The trick, the medicinal mixture of pain
And pleasure, worked every time at the Royal,
But now I've landed in a new hospital,
And it's hard to unveil your bits and pieces
To even the nicest of these new nurses.
Still a boy, I know some things have to be done,
And at least it turns out that I'm not alone,
For there's two big baths that the nurses have run,
And another boy wondering what he's done
Wrong to suffer this daily dose of torture.
I joke that we're blood-in-the-water brothers
As we're coaxed into the bubbling cauldrons.
Then, just as I start to wee-wee, it happens –
Rather than soaking in a bathtub turned red,
I'm astonished to see clear water instead!
I leap out of the tub like a scalded cat,
And grab a towel to cover my bare butt.

The nurses are clapping and laughing with joy,
But I'm feeling sorry for the other boy,
Who's sitting dumbstruck in a crimson hell-broth.
I will not blame him if he blackens my path.
I'm a lucky boy, and a happy one, too,
Now looking forward to my time at Lissue.
Another eight weeks, *another* eight weeks off
School! Compared to schoolwork, this should be a laugh.
    It takes just a wee while to settle well in,
To suss out the do's and the don'ts of the scene.
Like TV prison, there's a swapping system
That I quickly take a real interest in –
Smuggling stuff into the bogs and under
The walls that divide one bog from the other.
My most profitable client is Ivor,
Who, in a fit of sugar craze fever,
Lets me have the Ark Royal, ship of my dreams,
For two packets of Orange Chocolate Creams.
    Aptly enough, given his greeting jingle,
Ivor's one of only two guys who single
Me out for a late night dormitory fight.
The other's Damian, a cheeky wee shite
From the Shore Road, who bails out before the off.
But big Ivor's a game bird, though he's not tough,
And I reluctantly have it out with him,
In our pajamas, both in bare feet, 'fighting'
Over something that's forgettably silly.
I end up faking punches to his belly,
Unable to beat a friend about the head –
I might as well be wrestling a waterbed.
We end up covered in sweaty tears, not blood,
With our tested friendship better than good.
    Highlights of each week include Top of the Pops,
When us boys slither our way in for some bops
In the girls' dorm. Most nurses turn a blind eye,

As it's against the rules, knowing it's only
Flirty fun for pre-teens who couldn't dance to
Save themselves, and who wouldn't know what to 'do',
To be honest, if whatever 'the birds and
The bees' is really about was to up and
Land in our laps. Though some of us know, sadly,
More than we should of 'love' when it goes badly.
        Then there's the weekend weaving of the wicker
Baskets, a session with limited numbers,
Which, someway or other, I get roped into
Being part of. What starts as dejected boo
Hoos, turns into hat-high-in-the-air hoorays –
I'm a complete basket case come Saturdays.
        But it's not just a holiday camp. All play
And no work is not the order of the day.
We have bouts of school, too, in a room on site,
Though more often than not, we're out and about
On nature rambles in the countryside, where
We covet chestnuts and acorns, bird feathers,
Pale-blue speckled eggs, within earshot of trains
And in sight of the crowns of the Mourne Mountains.
        The chief routine glory of Lissue for me
Is the Santa's grotto of the toy room we
Get to play in regularly, set in a
Kind of miniature village, outside of the
Main house, spellbindingly full of every
Game and toy that we have ever dreamt to see.
With Monopoly and Subbuteo,
Working train sets, Johnny Seven Guns and Cluedo,
Plus some fancy games we had never heard of,
We vanish the days doing things that kids love.
        Convalescence complete, my Mum and Dad come
To bring me back to my box-room bed at home.
I came from a thin-walled, matchbox council house
With postage-stamp garden, with its humble fence

And latched gate put up to give our family
Some semblance of ownership and privacy,
To the gentrified House of Lissue, with its
Old world character and the voluptuousness
Of high-ceilinged places. All too soon, it's time
To say goodbye to Ivor for one last time.
Our friendship helped conquer my initial fears,
And leaves us standing in the playground in tears.

VI. Lookin' Out

We'd gather round the TV in those days of
Black-and-white to watch the tea-time news. We'd have
To catch up on the latest that the 'Troubles'
Had to offer – see who was flexing muscles
In the paramilitary arena.
Still early doors, but both the sides had seen a
Fair amount of bloodletting in their patches.
   I watch my dad sitting there as he watches
One of those round table discussions that were
Deemed discussions in name only, as they were
Favourite forums for war-jawing for all
Our politicians with backs against the wall.
There was no such thing as 'talks about talks' back
Then – just bake-to-bake bare knuckles; mighty craic
For people, in a black humoured kind of way.
It was Currie and Hume v Craig and Paisley –
Tag-team style – and when Cowan or Dunseith would
Ring the bell, pent-up viewers called out for blood.
   This night, amongst uncles, aunts and grandparents,
I see my dad get agitated. It is apparent
That his heckles have risen against 'Fenian
Lies and Popish propaganda' coming from
The tongues of Mr. Currie and Mr. Hume.
   I'm studying other faces round the room,
Seeing how they're soon in solid sympathy
With my proudly Protestant father's angry
Response to the Catholic politicians' rant –
All save my canny grandmother, who just can't
Stop smiling at my dad, the angrier he
Gets, which, when he catches on, is guarantee
That all hell will break out again between them.
What are you starin' at? And what's with the grin?
Oh, I'm just wond'ring why you're so red with rage.
We aren't smiling, but her smile would fill a page.
And then: *Just as sure as God is on His Throne,*

Just as sure as you were fostered from a Home,
Just as sure as your surname, it's in the eye
That they're your *born friends — it's lookin' outta ye!*

VII. The Alpha

It always has the promise of beginning,
Going down to the Alpha of an evening,
Rushing into the plush-pile, hoovered splendour
Of that well-carpeted cinema foyer,
An entrance large-postered with Hollywood greats
And lined with glassed counters for tickets and treats.
    Pop-corned and fizzy-drinked, we welcome the dark.
A torchy shines us to our seats. We shuffle-walk
Past half-risen fellow torn ticket holders
Who just conceal the narkiness that smoulders
Beneath their tightlipped smiles. We can't care less.
We're focused on our mission to see the best
That Hollywood has prepared for us tonight.
Subtly choosing seats, with 'best' mates left and right,
We elbow in to thole the advertisements,
Which merely serve to stoke our core excitement.
Anytime now, the magic curtains will close,
And though we are sitting, we'll be on our toes
For the lights to dim and the curtains to open.
And here it comes! The regal, roaring lion!
Calling us into the land of make-believe,
Which is somehow always better than where we live.
    Tonight, we're in the balcony, not the stalls,
So we get to pause and muster up the balls
To send our sticky lollies sky-rocketing
In the dark, raining down on the plebs below.
We snigger at the shouts and simply lie low,
Poker-faced in the torchlight that scans our row.
Then it's back to business and on with the show.
    This night, per usual, we're put through the mill,
Torn between laughter and tears, good and the ill,
But left believing that good guys always win.
There *will* be last minute punishment for sin.
The movie finishes, the titles descend,
And it draws to a close with two words: THE END.

But then that's just the start of the beginning,
For when we are young we are always winning.
The curtains close, and the Anthem begins, but
We're nowhere to be seen, being up and out
To round up the dregs of our pocket money
To bag us some chips from the Alpha café.
Then we run like the wind straight out the front doors
With our top-buttoned, hooded duffle-coat cloaks
Flowing behind us as we act out our scenes –
Full of Cowboys and Indians, Kings and Queens
Goodies and Baddies – in our innocent minds,
Realer than real ……. But we can't foresee the times
When the Alpha is a drinking den, drunken
Hoods being all the show, while true working
Men stay home to shelter their wives and children:
Not matinee men; but heroes, in the end.

VIII. Tour of Fire

Eleventh Night peaks. The Twelfth has come. Torches
Are lit and thrust into the driest branches
Of the pagan pyre. Time for the tour of fire.
Inferno in every window; wood and tyres
Sending smoke signals up into the night sky.
Proud Papal effigies preparing to die.
Bewildered Mormons, Jehovah Witnesses,
Looking down from their balcony maisonettes.
Loyal players in these fiery mirror-halls,
The usual suspects are fanning the flames:
The accordionist, the preacher, the drunk,
The skinhead, the hood, and the grammar school punk;
The flirt, the millie, and the token taig
(Suffered, good-humouredly, when things aren't too bad);
The dole-soul, the work-shy, and the work-is-done,
The mason, the slapper, and off-duty policeman;
All swaying and singing to Loyalist songs
Blaring from bass-booming home radiograms –
Some placed on the paths like musical coffins,
Tight owners sat on them, holding their half'ins.
   There are the beer-bellied boys, low-chested athletes,
Tenants tins stamped with girls in scant panties,
And their wives swigging their wee Smirnoff's and cokes,
Relaxing for the moment, sharing some jokes,
But secretly tuned to their man's rising laugh,
Some fearing the cost of this night's aftermath.
To drown such fears, there's Pernod and blackcurrant,
Leg-openers to maybe spare the children …
But all that's in the future, the night's still young,
Time for girlie banter about the 'well-hung' …
   Coffin-nail of choice is Embassy Regal –
Or Embassy Red if the wallet's able –
No. 6 or Players or Rothman's King Size
For highfalutin types with gold in their eyes,
Voluptuous women with bare bosom soufflés

Who know that their jiggle is mankind's heart-prize.
People suck on cancer sticks, long, hard and strong,
To raise themselves out of a houseful of wrong.
But let's give a nick to the Gallagher's weed
And return to the main act played on the green.
 To 'King' Billy and Bobby, and big Davy
Who'd savour the chance to mangle a Mickey.
They're seated around the 'top table', flanking
The main paramilitary man, who's yanking
Their chains with sinister banter to keep them
In check, making sure they're reminded it's him
That they owe loyalty to – lest they forget.
Not easy to do, considering the state
Of their mucker's face who had made the mistake
Of hitting the wrong guy a dig in the bake.
And there are plenty of youthful replacements,
Now sniffing round wee girls like dogs with two dicks:
Schoolgirls stretching their long chewing gum high wires
From hands to mouths, with confident, cheeky smiles,
Teen titties on show … but they don't realise
That their precious hymens are playing with fire.
Though some have clearly gone off to the races,
Those marks might be passion-poppies … or bruises …
Ack, you can't talk to them at this age! I hear
Big Sadie say, sidling up to bend my ear,
Reminding me to remember my teenage
Years, when such schoolgirls starred in my own wet dreams.
Then she smiles and suggests that we let them run on,
And pray that it amounts to no more than fun.
It's better than being alone like Ms. Ward –
Soaks her dildos in vinegar to keep them hard!
 But to get the whole truth, come a bit closer,
And witness the things surrounding love's bonfire.
See the innocent caught in the web of life,
Not one thing or other, not suited for strife,

Yet playing their part in the Protestant scene,
Being born in Rathcoole, and not Skibbereen.
Doubtless they're characters that carry some hope,
Who can look at their mates and dare to say, nope
That's not what I'm into, I mean no offense,
But hating a Catholic just makes no sense.
(But then that's easy when Republican guns
Are not pointed at your own flesh-and-blood ones.)
It's not all about Billy-boys, birds and booze.
There are ordinary heroes here because
It's their community, for good or for ill,
And they won't surrender their traditional
Celebrations totally to the dark side –
Would be easier to sit at home and hide.
See doting grandkids on grandparent's knees.
Hear the old ones swapping childhood memories.
Watch playground sweethearts holding hands in public,
Willingly running the wolf-whistle gauntlet.
See the 'deeps' in their duffle-coats sneaking
A joint, who can't for the life of them quite see
The point, but they've left their hippy incense-dark,
Unable to resist the communal lark,
For despite education's enlightenment,
They're still drawn to the Eleventh excitement.
    Whiff the irresistible aromas from
The welcome wagon-train of lay-by chip-vans,
Serving gravy chips, curry chips, fish suppers,
Pasties, sausages, bacon sodas, burgers,
Fanta, Coke, Iron Brew, Lilt, and Seven Up,
Ulster cheddar and cold cuts in big Belfast baps.
See kids queuing for cones from Mr. Whippy,
'99' pokes with flakes and chocolaty
Sprinkles, or flake-less but with tarn in top
Of strawberry or of raspberry syrup,
Or feasting on lollies like Seajet, Quencher,

Cornetto, Fab, Rocket, Magnum and Joker,
Choc Ice, Ice Pop, the ice-cream harmonica –
Wafered slabs of mouth-watering vanilla.
And Candy Floss! E number-less nebulas!
Pink pillars of creation where sugar's
Born! Formed by hands circling in widening gyres,
Kids crave second helpings of this edible air.
    (Love the banter between old primary school mates,
Now separated by 11-Plus Tests,
Swappin' slaggin's alongside the ice-cream van:
It's Strider the Slider & Vanilla the Man!
Without missing a beat, the ball's back with grins:
It's The Wallypops & The Skinhead Supremes!)
    The mobile shop that's a permanent fixture,
Is also getting well in on the picture,
Supplying the adults with mixers and cigs,
Mining the pocket money gold rush of kids
Who've struck it rich from half-blocked uncles and aunts.
With such dosh now burning a hole in their pants,
The shop is thankfully well-stocked and ready –
A cornucopia of confectionary!
There are Lucky Bags, Wine Gums, Chelsea Whoppers,
Sports Mixture, Black Jacks, Fruit Salad and Gob Stoppers,
Sherbet Fountains, Dib Dabs, Lucky Mines, Cola
Bottles, Flumps, Fruit Gums, Munchies and Mintola,
Fruit Pastilles, Fruitella and 10p mixes,
Bounty Bar, Golden Cup, Crunchie and Twix,
Galaxy, Picnic, Opal Fruits and Mars Bars,
Aero, Love Hearts, Caramel, Chocolate Éclairs,
Curly Wurly, Fry's Cream, Flake and Marathon,
Milky Bar, Milky Way, and the Toblerone!
As many sweeties as wild flowers of the Burren –
Don't have all night to stand here and name them …
(Keep those health-wise *tut, tut*'s in suburbia –
Sometimes these kids' only comfort is sugar.)

My granny and granda have just dandered up –
It's strictly Tetley tea in their drinking cups.
Salt-of-the-earth Ulster-Scots, country people,
Who carry the weather of their own locale
Like a breath of fresh air into this scene
And lend it some semblance of real dignity.
Granda's the quiet one, but granny's a talker
And though a churchgoer, nothing can shock her,
No, not even big Sadie and her harem
Of housewives come over to see how she's been.
    The fire's really raging by now, it's burning
Its way through the telegraph wires, and singeing
The eyebrows on reddening faces of folk
Too tipsy to care; and of proud kids who've built
The bonie and are innocently basking
In the glow of watching their parents' good time.
It's blistering paintwork on bonie-side homes
And fracturing windows in their living rooms.
But, like Christmas, Eleventh Night comes round just
Once a year: as then, so now, in God they trust
To foot the bill for any bonie damage,
Which won't be much as long as there's no rampage
Of eejit teenagers who can't hold their drink.
And to speak of some damage, I hate to think
Of blood spilled on the green before the night's out
But it happens, and's nearly always about
Someone caught putting their hands were they shouldn't.
It's always a clash with randy Protestant
Celebrity brethren blown in from Scotland
To add some Bannockburn to the Twelfth Day bands.
Their kilts and their sporrans can turn women's heads
And make them unmindful of their marriage beds.
It never ends well, but's mostly forgotten –
There's serious marching to do come morning.
    Let's leave the tour here at the height of the night;

Hope that the just will be allowed to sleep tight.
While, for some, it's all downhill from here to dawn,
For the young fire-builders, it's ladders to heaven –
It's hard to fathom, but part of the picture:
Kids are Cowboys and Indians, not just your
Prods versus Taigs of the grown-up condition.
The night truly begins for bonfire children
When the adults head off to parties or bed –
Time for baking big spuds in the dying red
Embers, and then feeding the flames to make
Sure that *their* bonfire survives until daybreak.
They've given their all for the Loyalist cause
Not with any prejudicial malice, as
Many of their parents and siblings have done,
But because they have been given permission
To be hunters and gatherers, selected,
Yes, by tribal grown-ups to help them erect
Monuments of Protestant magnificence,
But outside of flirting with fire, there's no sense
Of real premeditated, knowledgeable
Hatred directed through flames to those unable
To get housed by the Housing Executive –
At this stage, they're happy to live and let live.

IX. Bullets or Bats

Big Bobby Cain strolled down to The Diamond to
Seek some advice from one of the chosen few –
A Catholic solicitor that was allowed
To peddle his wares with the Protestant crowd
('Cause even the dogs knew that Taigs knew their rights).
    Ushered in by a cute wee thing in black tights,
And greeted by a smile and a handshake, he
Joked that the lawyer'd forgotten Masonry.
Grinning, the lawyer asked Bobby what he could
Do him for. Bobby then cleared his throat and said
That the lawyer might want to consider it
As being 'off the record', if he knew what
He meant. The lawyer then mimicked turning off
His recorder, and prepared to hear something rough.
    The form was that Bobby had made a mistake
That meant that both of his knees would have to break
Before his wrong could be put right. He had been
Out on the razzle one night at the Ardeen
Hall, and had drunkenly fell in with a doll
Who had never slept with her arse to the wall –
Problem being, she was married to his best
Mate, who was spending his time down in the Kesh
For giving his all for the Loyalist cause.
(It's easy to imagine the pregnant pause.)
His mate didn't give two shites for his hoor at home,
But such behaviour 'the boys' couldn't condone.
The lawyer leant forward and nervously asked
What exactly Bobby thought was his task.
    In a nutshell – in terms of the compensation,
Should he choose bullets or bats? So you can
Picture the look on the solicitor's bake –
A classic case of an oul Del Boy double-take –
As he slumped back bewildered into his chair.
Bobby understood that it was hardly fair –
The proverbial darkie's arse in moonlight –

To ask him the question, but in the light
Of the fact that a big payout was comin',
He thought the lawyer might fancy some action.
The lawyer 'hadn't heard the conversation',
But agreed to take a piece of the action.

    Bats over bullets was apparently best
To maximise coffers from the compo chest.
Though bullets were obviously dangerous,
The bats produced unpredictable messes,
And there'd be brownie points from the assessors
For extra trauma from hands-on aggressors.
So Bobby accepted the lawman's advice
And cast in his lot with bats' roll of the dice.
He phoned 'the boys' to pass on his decision,
And then went to bed with the television.

    Next day he was woken by his old mother
Who sensed that he was in some kind of bother
Because of the awkwardness of the nervous
Crew that had just interrupted her breakfast.
Bobby reassured her not to be worried,
And got into his daily duds and hurried
Downstairs to see who'd been sent to do the job –
He was relieved to see mates filling their gobs.

    There sat Mr. Red, Mr. White and Mr. Blue,
Three of the local smalltime hoods, sent round to
Administer Bobby's punishment beating.
The fact that the same doll had been giving
All three of them the same kind of attention
Was neither here nor there, not worth a mention –
The big lad's mistake was to go and get caught.
Feeling sorry for their oul mucker, they brought
Him some 'anesthesia' – gold whiskey, wine
And beer, and made him to promise, by the time
They'd return later that day, that he'd have them
Beaten down his fat neck to help numb the pain.

His ma was like a second mum to them all,
So he should pack her off to the bingo hall.
    He thanked them, though he worried that the booze would
Make him bleed a bit more, but they swore blind they'd
Get an ambulance the minute they were done –
There'd be no body when his mother got home.
They'd also take care not to leave a real mess,
To spare his mother any needless distress.
With all that being said, they showed themselves out,
And left their oul mucker to his drinking bout.
    To cut a long story short, they shattered his knees –
Three men who couldn't punch through wet paper bags …
But they kept to their word, for what it was worth –
He got help and survived by the skin of his teeth.
Once able, he hobbled out to cash his 'winnin's',
And was greeted by a gang of wee hallions
Who ran shouting round the shops, in Rathcoole rain:
Look at big Bobby, and his best mate – Cane!

X. Civility

Off-school summer days at Hazelbank Park,
Sun burnt sweaty from our frolics by the Lough,
Heading back, heads down, hungry enough for home ...
Then – cool civility on the polished lawn
Of the manicured bowling green from Heaven!
Daz-washed teams of working class men and women
In whiter-than-white duds and matronly frocks –
Most men sporting their pre-Fall, Sunday-best caps,
Most women topped with stylishly floppy hats –
Are rolling their perfectly weighted bowls that
Ride on Jesus-fish curves, each bowl traveling
On invisible beams round intervening
Planets to barely kiss the jack, or fired plum
Down the slick surface like a shot from a gun
To smack jack's pale face into the drop-off ditch.
Partitioned behind gated railings, we watch
And listen to banter as inherently
Necessary as the push to every
Bowl, bowls shaped like inflated vinyl singles,
With those many-coloured side-centered labels,
Lovingly buffed with magical cloths before
The taking of the mat, the balanced posture,
Arcing underhand swing (nothing down and low
About it despite the bias in the bowl),
And then the final flourish of the release
That leaves each hand open and at low-five peace.

XI. Heart Ache

Uniformed us, sweating in a mobile hut
Waiting for our English teacher to show up,
Dying to begin to torture the old fool:
Lucky 'Troubles' children, country grammar school
Kids who escaped from the massacre on a
Daily basis; bright teenagers who'd passed the
Eleven Plus test or, like *moi*, had fluffed it
But benefited from parents who'd paid out
Money they couldn't afford to try and make
Sure that we wouldn't copy their mistake
Of neglecting our precious education
For some quick nine-to-five remuneration:
Though few of them had been given any real
Choice – straight out to work was the working class deal.
　　Just as our undisciplined waiting almost
Reached its silly farm antics limit, he burst
In through the door like a man on a mission,
With mortarboard in hand and black gown swishing.
Immediately labeled a total twat,
He resembled a bald, bespectacled bat,
But swiftly secured a ripple of applause
By matching his bake to back end of a bus,
While claiming he knew not what he was doing.
Despite the fact that most of us were pissing
Ourselves at the dishevelled get-up of him,
He got himself together, quietened the din,
Commanded the front, closed his eyes and opened
His mouth, and booklessly waved a verbal wand.
　　He spoke of heartache, and numbness, and of pain;
Of what sounded like cold beer, good drugs, and wine;
Said stuff about dissolving, and forgetting,
In a place where there was no place for fretting …
The very classroom walls seemed to draw their breath
When he talked of almost being in love with death.

When teacher finished, he had no need to blush.
Coming round, out of the unreal teenage hush,
I turned and whispered to my mate beside me –
His mouth hanging open, his chin on his knee –
Wow ... what does he call that thing when it's at home?
Not sure ... but I think he said it was a ... 'poem'.
From that moment onward, there would be no doubt –
Liking poetry would be my 'coming out'.

XII. The Wide World

Not sure if I'm up with the lark, but I'm up
With my dad, who's swilling a final tea-sup
Before driving to his work in Swift's Kilroot,
A seven-to-three shift at the polymer plant.
It's going to be a sunny one, and I'm
Trying to be breakfasted and dressed in time
For a 'literary' morning with my mate
Marty from next door. We mustn't be late
For our rendezvous with our third wheel, mountain
Man Ian Rea, who might send us to detention
If we don't make religious Thoreau-time. Ian
Is two years older than us, and he's the brain
Behind our scrake-of-dawn adventure. Penguin
Paperbacks in hand, plan's to spend the morning
Down at Hazelbank, shore of Belfast Lough –
Amongst other things, famous for Paddy's Rock,
A giant boulder embedded on the beach.
Except at low tide, it is well out of reach,
But when the water retreats, it's a favoured
Spot for a photo opp. of children shouldered
Up on top by dads or big bruvs, all saying
Cheeeeese for smiling Kodak mums, who're capturing
An untroubled moment for the family
Album, such as it'll be. But this morning, we
Are on our ownios, three amigos who
Have waltzed down from the 'Coole, only stopping to
Lose our bridged faces in the cumulus smoke
Piped up by the old steam train taking a toke
For the ages on its way from Belfast to
Carrick to Larne, conjuring up Cat Ballou,
And Billy The Kid, The James Gang, and The Duke,
Silver screen idols straight from the only books
That my father ever leaves lying around
The house – those or the odd dirty secondhand
Magazines brought home from the late shift and 'left'

Lying bog-side as a wee fatherly 'gift'.
    The tide's well out, sun's up, and Paddy's Rock sits
Like a broken filling on the beach tongue. It's
A mind-boggler how it hasn't been renamed
'Billy's Rock' … The two shoreside turrets remain
Rooted like twin chessboard rooks, commanding the
Promenade. After a stroll up and down the
Shelly strand, we park ourselves on a bench seat
Initialled by paramilitary deadbeats
And their wenches, co-starring with ev'ry Ulster
Protestant acronym under the sun – four
'FTP' are only outdone by five 'KAI',
Rathcoole acronym for 'Kill All Irish'. I
Can never quite square that one with our Irish
Island locale … But it's a clear piece of pish
To some whom we've grown up with, those Billy Boys
Who pack the weekend stands for the Crues and Blues,
Who wouldn't know bold Jemmy Hope from Bob Hope,
Though they would find both men just as funny, no doubt,
If they did. The PIRA would make sure of that
By killing floating votes with gun, bomb and bat.
(The very name, 'KAI', was allegedly born
On the terraces at Ibrox Park, when some
Bright spark took a Danish striker's name and thought –
'I can make a cool gang name out of that!')
We've made our contribution to Protestant
Dissent by carving names alongside such rant,
Like Henry Joy McCracken and William Orr,
Presbyterians even we could die for,
And band names like Pink Floyd and The Grateful Dead,
The Rolling Stones, Led Zeppelin – wee Van! – instead.
    Our morning's chosen texts include Walden Pond
And the collected Keats. If we had a pound
For every Thoreau quote that hits the mark,
We teenage three would've a fortune in the bank.

'To live deliberately' – imagine thon!
Not blown about by every easy doctrine.
To 'stand on the shore of the wide world … and think …':
To think for ourselves, or at all! We would drink
A draught of Keatsian vintage to that, a full
Keg each of 'the blushful Hippocrene' an' all!
But we're the lucky ones, who've entered the world
Of books, enabled to weigh what we've been told
To believe in the balance of history…
Such are this morning's musings by the blue sea,
Under a blue sky, strong sea salt in the air.
We close the books, eye new ships steering for elsewhere.

XIII. Sprees

We used to go on stealing sprees in Belfast
Some Saturdays after sports. Sprees would last
Right up until the last door shut of the last
Shop. Truth be told, we tea-leafed for the blast
Alone, as most of what we knocked off wasn't
Worth its weight in gold, though gold watches wouldn't
Be sniffed at, even in the days before bling:
They could be sold or traded for the real thing –
LPs that your mates had half-inched before you
Had got the chance to nab. There were rogues' rules you
Had to follow or you'd find yourself looking
For another mob to cruise around with – like making
Sure cover was provided for your mates while
They parked in front of the LP racks to pile
Up their coveted 'collection' on the rack al-
Most deadeye-level with their wedding tackle.
    Two of us would casually wander in
To flank the main man so he could position
His selected stash for stealing. He'd open
His coat and pull up the jumper he'd put on
Especially for the job, press the LPs
To his chest, tuck the jumper into his jeans
And close his coat. Then he'd put his hands inside
His pockets to help take the weight, and decide
When was best to back out and head for the door.
In those days, security was so piss-poor –
Vinyl in sleeves was an invitation to theft,
And nothing would go beep beep beep as you left.
    I broke the record (predestined was the pun!)
For nicking most LPs on a solo run.
I smuggled nine LPs inside my duffle
Coat, and emerged to spark a major kerfuffle
On the bus back when my mates worked out that I'd
Swiped *Vince Hill Sings* by mistake. I nearly cried;
Those bastards just hee-hee-heed all the way home.

Not swapped or sold, we'd dump stuff that was stolen
So our parents couldn't question our 'purchase'.
But that LP didn't have to go to waste.
    It was my mother's birthday, and *Vince Hill Sings*
Was perfect – the only thing better was rings.
But when I lied and told my settee'd father
Of the 'gift', and he told me that my mother
Was upstairs sick in bed and would be chuffed to
Bits by my thoughtfulness, well what could I do?
I slowly climbed the stairs with a roast-red face,
And gave back her gentle smile, hid my disgrace,
And then retreated to my cell-like bedroom
To stare at the ceiling through the evening gloom.
Such evidence of 'sin' made it plain to me –
Even on stealing sprees, nothing comes for free.

XIV. The Skinhead and the Fag

Journeying one day from Rathcoole to Belfast,
He takes the Ulsterbus like the rest of us.
It is the height of the Wee Six's Troubles,
And his hard head is as bare as kids' bubbles.
Built like a brick shithouse, denimed, with skinners
And knee-length Doc Martens, he eyes us sinners
Like he is the Devil Himself. Myself and
The girl just absorb the intimidation,
And the older passengers never blink eyes.
He lights a Number 6 and turns to the skies.
By the time we reach the security gates
That ring the city centre, he's almost ate
A whole packet of fags, and lights another
As the soldiers board the bus to search for bother.
You either get off now or stay in your seat
Until the bus goes out through the other gate.
We're on our way to the Ulster Museum,
So we sit tight, along with the skinhead and
Two elderly women. But as the bus edges
Up Royal Avenue, the skinhead chances
His arm and stands up to ring the mid-door bell
To get off city centre. But we can tell
That the hardened bus-driver isn't going to
Play ball. What happens next's straight from Bellevue Zoo.
Mr. Skinhead, fag still in mouth, now decides
He'll open the door by himself, so he tries
To finger apart the black rubber middle.
At this stage, we are all starting to piddle
Ourselves at the impossibleness of his
No Surrender mentality, but he is
All the business, managing to get himself –
One shoulder, one arm, one leg – out from the shelf
Of the bottom step. Then, superhumanly,
He's born again, as (just) his bald pate snap-shuts free
Into a trapped liberty. I think that it's

Pure Belfast. The bus driver drives on. We sit
And wet ourselves. Wee millies and Buck Alecs
On the street run alongside, taking the piss –
Did yer fuckin' mummy stap tryin' to push?
We few on the bus feel his mortified blush.
As we pass out through the security gate,
The driver releases his angry inmate.
He just stamps out his fag-butt, without a word.
Wonder what shot will be heard around our world?

XV. The Hermitage

Saturday afternoon, with the rugby done,
Our hearts turn southward to the Kingdom of Mourne.
Rucksacks packed with tents, sleeping bags, bivvy bags,
Primus stoves, mountain clothes, shorts for swimming togs,
And with a shitload of bangers and baked beans,
Crusty bread, Kendal Mint Cake, too, we three teens
Board the Ulsterbus for Belfast bus station
Where we transfer for the trip through County Down,
A roller-coaster ride across drumlin land.
Disembarking seaside in Newcastle Town,
We scorn the easy bus ride to Bryansford
In favour of a machismo yomp instead.
    Almost running, like members of the Fellowship
Of the Ring, we reach Tollymore Forest Park.
Our own Rivendell! Our hobbit-haunted Shire!
Entering the pillared side entrance, we're
As awed as golfers on Magnolia Lane.
We have to get our tents up in case of rain
So we stride straight past the log cabin café,
Resisting the lure of the treat of the day,
Determined to make Skillen's Gate our base camp
Before the dusk sets in. 'Reaso' is the champ
At all things outdoors, and he soon cracks the whip
On Marty and me. You can't act like a tit
When Ian's in mountain mode. Skillen's Gate is on
The edge of the forest, foot of Luke's Mountain,
Suitably remote for three Thoreauians.
The park campsites are where the social craic is,
But they cost money, and we're low on shekels,
Plus we're much more interested in meadows,
And fresh water streams, and the quietness of stars,
Than being cooped-up with caravan campers.
    We pitch our tents on flat mattresses of ferns,
And while we cook up a storm, we take our turns
Foraging in the forest for wood to burn

On the campfire spot that we always return
To – the big beveled bowl of a hollowed-out
Tree stump holds another image of the night
Fires that the maker will relight in the sky.
With the blaze well built – and fed, like us – we're shy
Of making the backward trek to socialdom,
And vote to stay on the slopes of Luke's Mountain.
The night stars catch fire as we gather round ours
To swap stories of past forest adventures.

    The cloudless heaven-breast wears The Milky Way
Like a studded boxing belt taken from Day
As we wage memory-wars with each other.
We're high enough up to look down and over
The dark forest below us, spread out like a
Gigantic blanket between mountains and sea ...
With a swig from a final stream-chilled lager,
The last fireside recollection falls to me.

    From this vantage point, I can siphon the past
And follow the Shimna down through the forest
To The Hermitage, on a wilder than wild
Night, where Marty and I decided to hide
From an oceanic storm that had made us
Move from the mountain side: raindrops fell in droves
And the wind was wailing, banshee loud, so much
So that we lay gripped in giddy convulsions,
Holding on to the tent's sides, as it was set
To kite away if we let go. We laid bets
As to where it might end up if we did so,
And our own sides nearly split at 'Idaho'.

    But soon, we rung out the tent and sleeping bags,
Shouldered our rucksacks like sogging-wet teabags,
And beat a path to the home of the hermit:
A domed stone shelter beside the Shimna, that
Overlooks a deadly deep river-pause pool
(That has turned townie teenagers into fools).

That night The Hermitage was especially
Spooky, and we could safely assume that we
Were the only human souls tentless enough
To be bedding down in such a place. Short of
Being sluiced off the mountain like drowned puppies,
It was the only option left us 'Coolies.
    Night woods, when they're empty, are never as full,
And the sense of something is what we could feel
As we entered the dome and surveyed the scene.
Below us, the downpour made the black pool seem
A bubbling oil-broth stirred by someone unseen,
It's blistered face still mirroring the lightning
That threatened to frazzle the forest's long locks.
One pooled bolt seemed to rise out of the depths
Like the fantastic sword of a fabled king.
    Feeling there was no choice, we unpacked some things,
Just our sleeping bags, and orange bivvy bags
Which we frenchied over our dry sleeping bags
To beat the damp and the testicular cold.
We settled and bantered and tried to stay bold.
    But then came the sound of footsteps overhead
That sat us straight up in our bivvy bag beds.
We reached for our knives. Exhausted and baffled,
We stood up and listened hard for the muffled
Footsteps to sound again, cushioned by the earth
That topped the Shire-like dome. They came, back and forth
Across our roof, more human than animal,
Though the storm said we couldn't be sure at all.
The Hermitage having two ways in and out,
We split, and rushed up the steps with nervous shouts.
Then, for what seemed a long second, we saw him –
Shadow-clad, stock-still, bald head bowed, with his chin
On his chest, standing under an ancient oak –
Then he was gone. And with him went the storm that
Had brought us to that spot. We tried to rub him

From our eyes, but could not. So, with the wind
And rain stopped, we repacked our stuff and headed
Back up the path to Skillen's Gate and bedded
Down, again, on that edge between forest and
Hillside; that zone between deep leaf-dark and
The moonlit mountain, the road that we'd been on.
Rest of the night we slept with one eye open.
    Story ended, we just sit still, not speaking.
Above our heads, asteroids are etch-a-sketching
Across the blue star dome like criss-cross lovers,
While hares shape-shift between their holts and hovers
Under a moon so bright we'll need shades to sleep.
Stirring slowly, without a word, not a peep,
We douse the bowl of ashes and make for bed,
(Secretly dousing the demons in our head).
Then an angry rumble draws our eyes over
The low tree-line, down towards the distant seashore
Where deep purple clouds sound out their thunder song.
Seems the sea swell will curse the sky all night long.
We man up, hit the tents, and lay down the heads,
Confident the storm will run the coast instead
Of troubling us on the dry mountain side.
If not, we all know there's no place left to hide.

XVI. Verruca

Verruca …Verruca … sounds like a really
Fast car, doesn't it? Like Ferrari, I say,
That's what you're thinking of, isn't it, Ferrari?
Lenny laughs, silently. Says that's the crazy
Stuff that zooms around his head every day.
I smile and tell him that he's far from crazy.
We're parked in an empty shop doorway beside
Blinker's Café, looking out at Rathcoole wide
Boys and their UDA 'sponsored' black taxis.
The smoking black taxi men have only eyes
For the smoking hot Poly students who are
Waiting patiently in line in Bridge Street for
A taxi to ferry them to Jordanstown.
The girls giggle, or bow their heads to the ground,
Knowing they're ritual objects of desire.
It's a game of which the men will never tire.
Lenny rocks from foot to foot and asks me what
Degree I'm doing at the Polytechnic.
I tell him that I've told him a thousand times
Before: Bachelor's, Combined Humanities,
English major/Politics minor. He grins,
And tells me, again, to stick with my learnin's.
I know he fears that road-sweeping is my day
Job, when it's just a student summery way
Of making a rake of part-time quid to spend.
    As we're standing there, me with my brush in hand,
A flashy car pulls up next the taxi stand.
A strange man in a dapper suit gets out and
Makes his way towards Lenny and me, walking like
He owns the whole of Belfast. *It's only Mike,*
Lenny says, *don't let yourself be troubled. He*
Always comes around this time of year. Silly.
Coming from the 'Coole, I'm braced for anything,
But this man just saunters up to us, smiling,
And palms a small brown envelope to Lenny,

Who accepts it, humbly, without any eye
Contact, and slips it inside his overcoat.
The man thanks him, adjusts his tie at his throat,
Nods at me, and heads back to his limousine.
I look at Lenny like things aren't what they seem.
I know that he knows that I know it's money
That's in the brown bag that he thinks is funny,
So he mumbles that he's *keeping it for them*,
That *they give it to me to mind it for them*.
Turns out that Lenny is an authority
On the gee-gees, and rich guys regularly
Tap his tipster head for his horsey hunches.
Then, come race day, if his picks bring in bunches
Of green backs, the men in suits always drop off
A wee something in an envelope, and doff
Their caps to him for the knowledgeable nod.
But, strangest thing, Lenny couldn't give a sod
About his share of the winnings, and he laughs,
Again, says he's just keeping the money safe.
I'm tempted to laugh – Lenny's a tramp, a waif,
Homeless on the hard streets of Troubled Belfast.
If there's anyone who could do with some fast
Cash, it's him. He just looks at my question-mark
Face and grins, happy to keep me in the dark.

   He's the dead-ringer of the archetypal
Tramp, the kind that you might see in the local
Cinema in a Hollywood tearjerker
About the once successful, normal geezer
Who suddenly falls from grace, hits hard times,
Loses everything, including his mind,
But somehow manages to come back again,
Usually through the love of a good woman.
In Lenny's case, it's rumoured that a woman
Is to blame, though I haven't heard that from him.
They say he's an educated man from a

Respectable family, engaged to a
Girl who left him for someone else. He never
Recovered. Gave up his home. Ran for cover
To the roofless roads of Waring Street, High Street,
Lower North Street, Donegall Street and Bridge Street.
    Yes, he's the classic Beckettian cut of
A homeless man, an uncouth Jesus, in love
With uncleanliness – matted beard, matted hair,
Baggy coat, baggy shirt and baggy trousers,
And shoes that are boots but which sound like flip-flops
When he walks because their soles are hanging off.
And his skin is leather-like, and just as tough.
He's no beggar. Not that there's anything wrong
With that. He'll accept a sandwich or a warm
Styrofoam cup of tea or coffee from you,
But he won't proffer the empty cup for you
To drop your loose change into. That's not his thing.
He's not making a living doing nothing.
When he comes to die, he'll have more money than
You or I holed up in the Bank of Ireland,
Routinely salvaged from him by some honest
Local RUC men who knew about his
'Winnings'. Of course, he never uses a penny
Of it. Only penny he loves is Penny
Lane by The Beatles. He knows every Beatles
Song by heart. If he's not singing the praises
Of Tommy Stack and Lester Piggott, jockeys
Already legendary, or Nijinsky
And Arkle, equally legendary,
He croons the words of Lennon & McCartney
To himself, quietly, and word perfectly,
Songs like Hey Jude, Let It Be and Yesterday.
The irony of the lyrics aren't lost on
Him or me. We understand the life chosen.
And we know how it will likely end. It can't

End well. A homeless man has no retirement.
    Meanwhile, each summer holiday working day
I do my bit to love him in my own way,
And then leave him when it's time to head back round
To clock out at the Yard and catch the bus home.
Home for me's a family house in New Mossley.
His is a cold drunk-bastard-free shop doorway –
If he's lucky. If he's not, he's penny-free
And bloody-bruised in the mornings when I see
Him early. He says it's nothing, and it's not
Their fault, it's his, or the drink, or some such rot,
And my blood boils and I go have a wee word
With security gate men and am assured
That they'll look out for him again, as best they
Can, that they'll see that oul Lenny is ok.
Ah, Adrian, Patron Saint of Homeless Men!
Balls. Seen sweeping the streets is embarrassing,
So much so that at times I'm happy Lenny's
Beside me for carer credibility.
But my heart does go out to him, though it must
Be said that he's sorry for the likes of us,
Not condescendingly – flip sake, how could he? –
But, withdrawn from the merry-go-round, he sees
Us *rushing around the streets in a frenzy*
Of … what? Why all the hurry from A to B?
I haven't the heart to remind him of when
He would race to be spot on time for something
As simple as a quiet night with the girlfriend …
(He would cringe at our connection addiction …
But all that belongs in the present future –
It's time we got back to Lenny's *Verruca*.)
Could be a good name for a fast car or a
Fast horse … Lenny nods, and reminds me of the
Reason we started on our conversation.
Your da's 'low-chested athlete's a good'un,

But imagine them calling those oul things 'Athlete's
Foot'? I'm no sprinter, and sure they're on my feet
And hands and probably elsewhere! I point out
That athlete's foot and plantar warts are no joke,
And that left untreated are a mosaic
Of trouble and pain. He smiles. Calls me 'Wissac-
Issac'. But agrees to let me bring some cream
For his 'wee wart mosaic' in the morning.
He peers at passing people, swigs cold coffee,
Then gets lost in the singing ... *She loves you, yeah,*
Yeah, yeah, she loves you, yeah, yeah, yeah, she loves you,
Yeah, yeah, yeah, yeah ... and with a love like that, you ...

XVII. Sniper

God love the family from the Culmore Road
Who owned a huggable wee dog that they called
Sniper. *Sniper! Sniper!* They'd loudly sing-song.
At the time, Sniper could do no earthly wrong.
He was christened in the crisis produced by
Trigger-happy Paras on Bloody Sunday.
Then, the family had no hesitation
In calling him in from their Republican
Cul-de-sac of Derry's Catholic Culmore.
Indeed, they'd volunteer to stand at the door
In full public view to summon the Sniper.
They hollered his name with parade ground power
And Sniper would hear and scamper homewards
To be showered with head pats and big belly rubs.
　　Right up and through the years of the hunger deaths
They polished the medals on his doggy chest.
But even the Troubles couldn't hold its heat.
When sectarian tides began to retreat
Certain things became decidedly dodgy
As the area became more upwardly
Mobile. Mixed middleclass families began
To settle into Sniper's Culmore kingdom,
Bringing pedigree hounds out onto the grounds
To help harry the postmen on postal rounds.
Gradually, his owners grew shy to call
Sniper in by name. Tactfully, it was all
About playing to their prosperous neighbours
And 'Sniper' sounded classless to monied ears.
　　Sniper? Sniper? What on earth had possessed them?
As good Catholics, could they live down the shame?
Every time they had to call the dog in,
They would cup their mouths, whisper his name like sin,
Repeating *Sniper, Sniper, here boy, come here.*
And knowing no better, he'd always appear.
Caught in the cross-sights of respectable types,

Target of stares across avenues and drives,
In danger of lowering the area's
Tone, cutting the price tag on their new neighbour's
Homes, they couldn't be guilty of such a thing
In a community where money was king.
Did Sniper feel rejected? Did he feel blue?
Think why weren't they hollering like they used to?
Maybe he mused as he came in off the streets
On why whispered calls came with more doggy treats.
   But if this teaches anything of value –
Naming in anger can come back to bite you –
Today, it need hardly be said, that you need
A dog called Sniper like a hole in the head.

XVIII. Flags

Flags, fucking flags …
What real use have they ever been to anyone?
Oh yeah, we've marched behind them
Plenty of times, but save to wrap our proud
Big-bellied patriotic selves up in, what else?
Waste of fucking time, waste of fucking cloth,
If you ask me …

Raised with the results of patriot bragging,
I have always been wary of flag-waving.
Going into an American classroom
To talk to some children about where I'm from,
I notice the Irish tricolour hanging
Print-new and proudly from the classroom ceiling.
It's natural to assume I'm from Ireland.
How do I explain about Northern Ireland?
As a holder of both passports from back home
(Dissenting attempt to annoy everyone)
I am determined to keep my big mouth stum.
Why bother splitting history hairs with children?
But soon as the beaming teacher stretches out
Her hand in confident welcome, I blurt out
That the flag isn't the flag of my country.
At first she thinks that I'm just being funny,
But I gently insist that the flag is wrong.
Befuddled embarrassment, agitation,
Summarises the look on the teacher's face,
But I tactfully stress that if I'm to teach
The children, accurately, about where I'm from,
She'll have to accept that the flag is … well … wrong.
    To put things, technically, on the right track
I say that the flag should be the Union Jack.
Seeing another huge question mark take her face,
I speak of the red, white and blue, the British
Flag of T-shirt fame, of Buckingham Palace,

And suddenly she's back in her happy place,
Promising me that the Union Jack will soon
Be flying in full glory in the classroom.
I feel guilty, worried about the hassle,
The expense, but she sees it's a teachable
Moment and reassures me that it's okay.
    I return to the school the very next day
To find the mischief-makers hung side by side.
It then becomes clear I've still got to decide
How to fairly present wee Northern Ireland
Without draping another flag beside them –
The red-handed standard of the Ulstermen.
Feels ridiculous making the suggestion,
But poor teacher runs with it, claiming it shall
Be no problem swinging a third flag at all.
On my last visit, just a few days later,
There hangs the full blood-handed flag of Ulster,
Centre stage in the troublesome trinity:
Perfectly appropriate, it seems to me,
Given Ulster's piggy-in-the-middleness
From one British-Irish conflict to the next.
The flags are my visual three point sermon
As I attempt to educate the children.
Who's to know if anything makes sense to them?
If not, it isn't for the want of trying.
    I joke on the phone with a friend back home
That the flags are eenie meenie miney, min-
Us moe. He laughs, but tells me I'm getting slow
If I think I can get away without moe.
There's a fourth flag needed for the equation
To list all the flags of the Ulster Question.
I have forgotten the nine county, not six,
Version of Ulster's banner – red hand, red cross
Set against a bright yellow, not white, background –
A flag fit for flying in Donegal Town.

Tempted to further enlighten the teacher,
I've a hunch my messages mightn't reach her.

Our mutual sectarian alchemies,
Which changed green, white and orange
Into green, white and gold,
Made real political progress seem
As allusive as the old philosopher's stone.
Sure it would've been easier to find a fart
In a field of flags, fart-flapping
On a blustery Ulster morning, than to imagine
Us ending up with 'The Chuckle Brothers'.

XIX. Budgie

Drive the Demon of Bigotry home to his den,
And where Britain made brutes, now let Erin make men!
— from 'Erin' by William Drennan (1754-1820)

It seemed like every single house had one
Except us, though we had an aquarium,
The other housed comfort of the working class,
One behind the bars, the other behind glass.
I thought it odd that the underprivileged
Would happily keep something tanked or caged,
Considering our hard human condition.
I guessed it was our identification
With creatures as poorly predestined as we
Often believed our hand-to-mouth selves to be.
Keeping birds in seed is a real kind of love,
And sprinkling fish-flakes like manna from above.
     Now by a strange quirk of imagination —
Some new light from within, something gene-given —
Every time I saw a map of Ireland
I rebelled against the usual notion,
The birds-eye, map-driven visualisation
Of Ireland backed to the masculine mainland,
Her leafy petticoats eyed-up for stripping,
Her feminine fields ripe for penile ploughing.
Even as a child, I refused to see it
As a victim, back-turned towards Brit-
Ain, inviting colonial rear-ending.
I saw it as a battling budgie, facing
The mainland, proudly, prepared for what might come
Winging over the waves from the gauntlet realm.
Though couched by Drennan to properly provoke
His fellow Irishmen to throw off the yoke,
It was no 'base posterior of the world',
Arsehole waiting to be slavishly buggered
By a foreign foe even our side flinched at.
No more servile hung'ring for the 'lazy root',
But male and broad-shouldered as The Hill of Caves —
Where the United Irishmen first swore slaves
Would be set free by jointly overturning

The home-based kingdom of the sectarian –
Our bold-hearted budgie had come of age,
Had climbed the ladders and looked in the mirrors,
Then ignored the dudgeon doors and bent the bars,
Self-paroled, assuming independent airs.
    So turned towards the royal raven of England,
To my mind, our Irish budgie was crowned
With the head of Ulster: the tufty hair of
Wind-blown Donegal, the brawn and brains of
Radical Belfast, the 'Athens of the North',
With the clear blue eye of Neagh, and beak of Ards,
Heart, lungs and Dublin barrel-bulge of Leinster,
The fiery feet and claws of mighty Munster,
And thrown-back western wings of mystic Connaught.
Four provinces, four-square, forever landlocked,
Friend of brother Celts, but full of righteous rage
Against the keeper of the keys to the cage,
The Bard's 'blessed plot', his 'precious stone set in
The silver sea', his 'dear, dear land', his England.
Yes, no Catholic cage, nor Protestant pound,
Could hold my dissenting ideal of Ireland.
For in spite of spite, it was Drennan's Eden,
'In the ring of this world the most precious stone!'
His 'Emerald of Europe', his 'Emerald Isle'
Which no vengefulness would finally defile.

ADRIAN RICE is from Northern Ireland. He was born just north of Belfast, in Whitehouse, Newtownabbey, County Antrim. He graduated from the University of Ulster with a BA in English & Politics, and MPhil in Anglo-Irish Literature. He has delivered writing workshops, readings, and lectures throughout the UK & Ireland, and America. His first sequence of poems appeared in *Muck Island* (Moongate Publications, 1990), a collaboration with leading Irish artist, Ross Wilson. Copies of this limited edition box-set are housed in the collections of The Tate Gallery, The Boston Museum of Fine Arts, and The Lamont Library at Harvard University. A following chapbook, *Impediments* (Abbey Press, 1997), also earned widespread critical acclaim. He edited *Signals* (Abbey Press, 1997), which was a London *Times Educational Supplement* "Paperback Choice." He has also edited five anthologies of children's poetry, art and drama. In 1997, Rice received the Sir James Kilfedder Memorial Bursary for Emerging Artists. In autumn 1999, as recipient of the US/Ireland Exchange Bursary, he was Poet-in-Residence at Lenoir-Rhyne College, Hickory, North Carolina, where he received "The Key to the City." His first full poetry collection, *The Mason's Tongue* (Abbey Press, 1999), was shortlisted for the Christopher Ewart-Biggs Memorial Literary Prize, nominated for the Irish Times Prize for Poetry, and translated into Hungarian by Thomas Kabdebo (*A Komuves Nyelve*, epl/ediotio plurilingua, 2005). In 2002, he co-edited a major Irish anthology entitled, *A Conversation Piece:*

Poetry and Art (The Ulster Museum in association with Abbey Press). His latest publications include *The Tin God*, a history of Cans Metal Box factory, Portadown, which was shortlisted for the "Celebrating Our Local History" Competition by the Northern Ireland Publications Resource; and *Insights* (as editor), an anthology of poetry from The Dungannon Visually-Impaired Group, which earned the Dungannon & South Tyrone Borough Council's "Achievement Award." His poems and reviews have been broadcast internationally on radio and television, and have been published in several international magazines and journals, including *Poetry Ireland Review, The Echo Room* and *The New Orleans Review*. Selections of his poetry and prose have appeared in both *The Belfast Anthology* and *The Ulster Anthology* (Ed., Patricia Craig, Blackstaff Press, 1999 & 2006) and in *Magnetic North: The Emerging Poets* (Ed., John Brown, Lagan Press, 2006). A chapbook, *Hickory Haiku*, was published in 2010 by Finishing Line Press. Rice returned to Lenoir-Rhyne College as Visiting Writer-in-Residence for 2005. Since then, he and his wife Molly, and baby son, Micah, have settled in Hickory, where he teaches English and Creative Writing at Catawba Valley Community College and Appalachian State University. Turning poetry into lyrics, he has also teamed up with Hickory-based and fellow Belfastman, musician/songwriter Alyn Mearns, to form "The Belfast Boys," a dynamic Irish Traditional Music duo. A debut album, *Songs For Crying Out Loud*, was recently released.

PSALM 103 v. 12-22

Cover artist **JON TURNER** grew up in Worcestershire, in the English countryside, and studied English Literature at Balliol College, Oxford University before pursuing a career in art and design. Now living in Manchester, his pen and ink drawings aim to combine a literary sensibility with a surreal sense of mystery. Examples of his work can be found at www.thisisjonturner.com.

CPSIA information can be obtained
at www.ICGtesting.com
Printed in the USA
FFOW02n1314280414
5084FF

9 781935 708995